THE ENLIGHTENED BUSINESS ANALYST

Empower your career and transform your approach towards business challenges

Anupamm Singh

INDIA • SINGAPORE • MALAYSIA

ISBN
Paperback: 979-8-89475-292-1
Hardcase: 979-8-89498-355-4

Contents

Contents

Acknowledgements

❖

I would like to express my heartfelt gratitude to my wife, Shaveta, and my kids, Prisha and Riya, for their unwavering love, support, and understanding throughout the journey of writing this book. Your patience, encouragement, and belief in me have been the driving force behind my pursuit of this dream.

Shaveta, your constant encouragement and steadfast support have been my anchor. From the late-night writing sessions to the moments of self-doubt, your unwavering faith in my abilities kept me going. Your love and understanding provided me with the strength to persevere, and your insights and feedback have been invaluable. You have been my confidante, my cheerleader, and my rock. Thank you for being by my side through every step of this journey.

Prisha and Riya, your innocent smiles and endless curiosity have been a source of inspiration. Watching you grow and learn has reminded me of the importance of persistence and the joy of discovery. Your patience, even when I was engrossed in my writing, showed a level of understanding beyond your years. The moments of laughter and joy we shared were a refreshing break from my work and gave me the energy to continue. Thank you for your unconditional love and for bringing so much happiness into my life.

Your presence has been a constant source of strength and inspiration, reminding me of what truly matters in life. This book is a testament to your love and support. Thank you for standing by me through the ups and downs, for cheering me on during the challenging moments, and for celebrating with me during the moments of triumph. This book is as much yours as it is mine, and I am deeply grateful for your love and unwavering support.

Preface

Welcome to "The Enlightened Business Analyst," a journey of discovery, growth, and self-realization in the world of business analysis. In this book, we invite you to embark on a transformative adventure alongside our protagonist, a young graduate navigating the complexities of the professional world.

Business analysis is not just about gathering requirements or analyzing data; it is a journey of self-discovery and personal growth. Through the protagonist's experiences, readers will gain valuable insights into the challenges and rewards of this dynamic field and uncover the true essence of what it means to be an enlightened business analyst.

As you journey through these pages, you will encounter moments of frustration, flashes of insight, and opportunities for growth. Alongside the protagonist, you will explore the core components of business analysis – from processes and systems to data – and discover how each contributes to the overall success of an organization.

But beyond the technical aspects, this book delves into the deeper meaning of enlightenment — the realization of one's true purpose and potential. Through the protagonist's journey, readers will be inspired to embrace their own path to enlightenment, finding fulfillment and purpose in their professional endeavors.

"The Enlightened Business Analyst" is more than just a book; it is a roadmap to personal and professional growth. Whether you are a seasoned business analyst or someone embarking on a new career path, this book offers valuable insights and practical lessons to help you unlock your true potential and achieve success in the ever-evolving world of business analysis.

So, join us on this captivating journey of self-discovery and growth, and uncover the secrets to becoming an enlightened business analyst.

The New Business Analyst

In the bustling city, John Smith, a fresh graduate with a degree from a prestigious university, stood across the street from the doorstep of a leading technology company. The large signage on the top of the building showcased its grandeur and the prestige it brought to people's careers. The shiny title of "Graduate Analyst" awaited him inside, but doubts clouded his fresh-out-of-school mind.

The sleek glass façade of the building loomed before him, reflecting the morning sun and casting a brilliant glow on the street below. The signage above, bold and imposing, spoke of success and opportunity, a beacon for ambitious minds like John's. This was his first day at a company renowned for its innovation and cutting-edge technology.

As he stepped inside, the atmosphere changed. The air-conditioned lobby was a sharp contrast to the city's summer heat, and the sleek, modern interior exuded an aura of professionalism and high stakes. Colleagues zipped past him, immersed in conversations filled with tech jargon and project updates. The open office layout buzzed with the hum of computers and the soft clatter of keyboards. Digital screens displayed streams of code and intricate project timelines, a testament to the company's high-paced environment.

John approached the reception desk, where a friendly receptionist handed him his ID badge. Clipping it to his shirt, he took a moment to absorb his surroundings. The walls were adorned with the company's milestones and achievements, each framed article and award reinforcing the prestige that the signage outside had promised.

Guided by an HR representative, John navigated through a maze of cubicles and meeting rooms, each space occupied by focused professionals. He couldn't help but feel a mix of awe and intimidation. This was a far cry from the structured environment of his university.

Finally, he reached his designated workspace. It was modern and minimalist, with a sleek monitor and a keyboard that seemed to promise endless possibilities. His desk, though small, was strategically placed to offer a view of the bustling office, a constant reminder of the dynamic world he was now part of.

As he settled into his chair, the reality of his new role began to sink in. The shiny title of "Graduate Analyst" was no longer just a label; it was a responsibility. He was expected to contribute, to innovate, and to thrive in this competitive environment. The journey from academia to the corporate world had begun, and with it came the challenges and opportunities he had long anticipated.

John took a deep breath, pushing aside his doubts. He reminded himself of the journey that lay ahead, a tale of growth, learning, and discovery in the uncharted territory of the tech world. The path was filled with potential pitfalls and opportunities for growth, and he was ready to tackle them head-on.

His mind drifted back to the university halls where he had spent countless hours poring over textbooks and attending lectures. The structured environment of the classroom had shaped his intellect, filling him with knowledge. However, as he stood in this corporate jungle, he couldn't help but wonder if those classes had truly prepared him for the complexities of the real world. He remembered the late nights in the library, the heated discussions in study groups, and the detailed notes he meticulously prepared for exams. The familiarity of that academic routine had been comforting, a predictable rhythm of learning and assessment.

However, as he stood in this corporate jungle, surrounded by the hum of industry and the buzz of innovation, he couldn't help but wonder if those classes had truly prepared him for the complexities of the real world. The transition from theory to practice seemed daunting. The challenges here were not about passing exams but about making real-world decisions, solving actual problems, and contributing to live projects that could impact the company's success. The safety net of academic life was gone, replaced by the high stakes of the corporate environment.

As John settled into his chair, he felt the weight of expectations pressing on his shoulders. He was no longer a student but a professional expected to contribute to a thriving technology company. The gap between his academic knowledge and the practical skills needed in this corporate environment seemed vast.

His thoughts were interrupted by the arrival of his mentor, a seasoned analyst with years of experience. The mentor's encouraging words echoed in John's mind: "You've finished your courses and earned that degree, but now, you're like a blank canvas in the tech world. You're a generalist on Day 01, trying to figure out where your strengths lie in the vast landscape of analytics."

The mentor continued, "Your theory classes might not be the guiding stars right now. You're stepping into a hands-on journey, where the theories you memorized may need a bit of a twist to fit the real-world puzzles."

With a gentle smile, the mentor added, "But hey, if you paid attention in those theory classes, if you absorbed the techniques like a sponge, you might find some gems to leverage. It's time to giddy up, John! You're not expected to be a pro from the get-go. You're a blank slate, and this profession is about to paint your story with experiences, challenges, and triumphs."

John took another deep breath, feeling a mix of excitement and nervousness. The corporate jungle stretched before him, and he embraced the uncertainty of the journey ahead. The mentor's words echoed in his mind—giddy up, John, for the tech profession is about to take you on a ride of a lifetime.

In the ensuing days, John found himself knee-deep in the corporate whirlwind. His first assignment played hard to get, teasing him from a distant horizon. Before diving into the hands-on world of business analysis, he had to navigate through a maze of internal training courses, policies, and procedures.

The training rooms echoed with the hum of presentations and the rustle of complex documents. John spent hours poring over intimidating files containing the company's grand vision and mission. As he delved into the intricacies of these seemingly cryptic statements, the corporate puzzle slowly began to unravel.

Complicated diagrams, flowcharts, and jargon-filled paragraphs stared back at John from the pages. "Is this really necessary?" he wondered, feeling a bit overwhelmed. But as his mentor had hinted, this was just the warm-up before the real race.

Then came the grueling assessments, designed to test the depth of his understanding. John faced a barrage of questions that dissected the contents of those intimidating documents. It wasn't just about reading; it was about comprehending, absorbing, and applying the essence of the company's philosophy.

With each assessment, John felt the weight of responsibility settling on his shoulders. The blank slate was being etched with the ink of knowledge and practical understanding. He slogged through the assessments, determined to prove his mettle in the face of complexity.

As the weeks rolled by, John trudged through the training, feeling a mix of anticipation and trepidation.

The elusive first assignment lingered on the horizon, and he knew that every assessment, every policy he grasped, was a stepping-stone toward the hands-on journey that awaited him in the world of business analysis.

Chapter 02

The First Assignment

On a typical morning, at precisely 8:50 am, John walked into the city office following his usual routine. The streets were already bustling with commuters, each lost in their own thoughts. As he made his way through the familiar route, passing by the corner coffee shop and the newsstand, he noticed the subtle shifts in the city's rhythm—the barista's cheerful greeting, the aroma of freshly brewed coffee, and the crisp pages of the morning newspaper being flipped by hurried readers.

Yet today was different. Despite the familiar rhythm of his steps, there was a subtle change in the cadence of his enthusiasm. It wasn't that John lacked eagerness for work; rather, a quiet discontent lingered, fueled by the feeling that the knowledge he craved had eluded him. The city's energy, which once invigorated him, now felt somewhat detached from his own inner stirrings.

As he approached the towering glass building of the tech company, its large signage gleaming in the morning light, he felt a familiar mix of awe and apprehension. The revolving doors ushered him into the bustling lobby, where the air-conditioned breeze provided a stark contrast to the city's warmth outside. Colleagues hurried past, their conversations a blend of casual banter and serious discussions about ongoing projects.

The air in the office hummed with the usual sounds of ringing phones and the click-clack of keyboards. John greeted the receptionist with a nod and scanned his ID badge at the security turnstile. As he rode the elevator up to his floor, he watched the numbers light up sequentially, each ding a reminder of the structured routine that awaited him.

Stepping out onto his floor, John was greeted by the sight of his coworkers already immersed in their tasks. The open office layout buzzed with activity, yet within John, a sense of anticipation lay dormant. His aspirations, his hunger for learning, had not found fulfillment in the corporate world so far. The rows of cubicles, the endless meetings, and the daily grind of minor tasks felt repetitive and uninspiring.

John's desk, neatly organized with his monitor and keyboard, stood as a silent witness to his growing frustration. He yearned for more than the learning assignments that had become part of his daily work routine. He longed for projects that would challenge his intellect and allow him to apply the vast knowledge he had acquired during his university years.

As he settled into his desk, glancing at the clock ticking away, John couldn't shake off the tinge of disappointment. It wasn't about a lack of commitment or interest; it was the yearning for something more, something directly tied to his passion for business analysis. The daily grind of training and learning activities had started to lose their appeal, leaving him with a subdued spirit. Despite consistently scoring high marks on his assessments, often achieving perfect scores, he felt unchallenged and unfulfilled.

It had been almost six weeks since he joined the company, and the initial excitement had given way to a sense of monotony. While shadowing colleagues and attending briefing sessions provided occasional glimpses into real-world applications, these experiences were few and far between. Invitations to social clubs and team events were pleasant diversions, but they did little to stimulate his analytical mind.

Through the office windows, the city buzzed with life, and John sat amidst it, contemplating the day ahead. The routine tasks waited, but the spark of curiosity, the desire to dive into the realm of his chosen field, remained unignited. He yearned for assignments that would truly challenge his skills and allow him to apply his knowledge in meaningful ways.

Little did he know that the day held surprises, challenges, and perhaps the turning point he needed to reignite the flame of excitement within him.

John was going through his usual New Starter checklist, double-checking if he had missed any tasks or actions. He was contemplating the uneventful morning when a soft chime resonated from his computer.

An email notification blinked on his Outlook, instantly drawing his attention. The sender's name, unfamiliar to John, intrigued him—Process Peters. Who could this person be?

With a swift click, John delved into the company's active directory system, unraveling the mystery behind the name. As the screen displayed Process Peters as one of the lead Subject Matter Experts (SMEs) within his division, a spark of anticipation flickered within John. This was no ordinary email, and Process Peters held a significant role.

A sense of happy anxiety settled in as John opened the email. The words on the screen hinted at a new chapter unfolding in his corporate journey. He read that he had been assigned to Process Peters' team on secondment, a term that stirred both excitement and curiosity. What did this mean for him?

The email provided a teaser, stating that a meeting invite would follow shortly. John couldn't help but wonder about the tasks and expectations that awaited him on this unexpected detour. Process Peters, with his enigmatic name, seemed to hold the key to a realm beyond the routine.

As John pondered the possibilities, the meeting invite popped up on his screen. The subject line hinted at a deep dive into tasks and expectations. A mix of nervousness and anticipation settled within him. Little did John know that this unexpected turn in his day would be the catalyst for the learning adventure he had been yearning for, propelling him into a new chapter of challenges and growth.

With the meeting set for 11:00 am, John found himself with approximately two hours of anticipation before the veil would be lifted on the true meaning of this unexpected secondment. A mix of curiosity and eagerness lingered in the air as John pondered the upcoming encounter.

Deciding to make the most of this interim period, John resolved to dive into some research and prepare himself for whatever lay ahead. The challenge, however, was that he wasn't entirely certain what, precisely, he was preparing for. The ambiguity of the situation injected a dose of uncertainty into his efforts. Yet, undeterred, John pressed on, determined to glean as much information as possible within the limited time frame.

His computer screen became a canvas for exploration as he navigated through documents, internal resources, and anything that could potentially shed light on the tasks and expectations awaiting him. The clock ticked away, each passing minute heightening the suspense.

As John immersed himself in the task at hand, the uncertainty that initially tinged his efforts began to transform into a sense of quiet confidence. It was a journey into the unknown, but armed with the willingness to learn and adapt, John was ready to face whatever challenge awaited him.

The city outside continued its bustling rhythm, oblivious to the transformative moments unfolding within John's workspace. Little did he know that these next two hours would set the stage for a pivotal chapter in his journey as a Business Analyst.

As John delved deeper into the sea of information, he felt the waves of confusion and exhaustion slowly washing over him. The more he tried to grasp, the more elusive clarity became. Nearly 30 minutes of browsing through mounds of content left him mentally drained, prompting him to rise from his chair.

In search of solace, John walked to the nearby window, gazing at the city skyline. Frustration mingled with fatigue as he questioned his approach. "What am I doing wrong? This is supposed to be fun. Why am I getting exhausted?" The weight of the unknown loomed large, casting a shadow over the excitement he had initially felt.

In this moment of introspection, the wise words of his mentor surfaced in his mind like a guiding light.

It was a revelation that sparked a sudden jolt of clarity within John. He had been chasing after an ocean of knowledge, attempting to consume too much in too little time. The path to understanding, he realized, lay in simplicity. With newfound determination, he hurried back to his desk, ready to realign his approach.

Seated once again at his computer, John began to draft a document. Instead of drowning in the complexity, he focused on his fundamentals, breaking down the information into manageable chunks. The fog of confusion lifted, revealing a clearer path ahead. Little did John know that this return to basics would not only ease his overwhelm but also set the stage for a more fruitful engagement with the challenges that awaited him in the meeting with Process Peters.

WORDS OF WISDOM

"When inundated with information, or when you feel the world around you seems too complicated, go back to your fundamentals. Stick to the basics."

– Anupamm Singh

John's Learning Journal

Armed with a renewed perspective, John sat down to craft a document tailored to his own learning journey. He realized that most of his knowledge rested in the theoretical realm, a foundation that needed practical scaffolding. With this insight, he began jotting down pointers, aiming to bridge the gap between what he already knew and what he needed to learn.

Aware that his interpretations were subjective, John adopted a simpler and methodical approach. He decided to first acknowledge his existing understanding of the task or situation and then conceptualize it within the framework of his current knowledge. The key, he reminded himself, was to stay open to adjusting these details as he navigated the practical landscape.

Fingers tapping away, John initiated his research with a specific focus. He typed into his web browser, "What is a Subject Matter Expert." The search results unfolded a plethora of definitions, articles, and insights. However, armed with his newfound approach, John filtered through the information with a discerning eye.

As he absorbed the content, John began to distill the complexities into simple, digestible nuggets of understanding. The act of writing allowed him to articulate his thoughts, creating a structured foundation for learning. Each sentence became a stepping stone, leading him away from the overwhelming maze of information and towards a clearer comprehension of the subject at hand.

John's Learning Journal

Subject Matter Expert

A Subject Matter Expert (SME) is an individual who possesses extensive knowledge and expertise in a particular field or subject. The role of an SME is to provide in-depth insights, guidance, and specialized information to aid decision-making, problem-solving, or project implementation within that specific domain.

Key Aspects of an SME

- SMEs are highly knowledgeable in their specific field, often possessing deep expertise that comes from years of experience, education, or practical application.

- They contribute to solving complex problems within their area of expertise, offering valuable insights and perspectives that others may not have.

- SMEs assist in decision-making processes by providing relevant information, analysis, and recommendations based on their specialized knowledge.

- SMEs often play a role in training and mentoring others within their field, sharing their expertise to help develop skills and understanding among colleagues or team members.

- They collaborate with cross-functional teams, acting as a bridge between technical details and broader business objectives, ensuring that decisions align with the intricacies of their subject.

Little did John realize that this meticulous process of breaking down complex concepts would serve as a compass, guiding him through the intricate terrain of Business Analysis. His document, initially intended for personal learning, would gradually transform into a roadmap for navigating the challenges that lay ahead in his newfound role.

With a newfound grasp of the Subject Matter Expert's (SME) role, John turned his attention to identifying the gaps in his understanding. Although he could anticipate what to expect from Process Peters in terms of functions, the practical application remained elusive. To maximize the upcoming meeting's potential, John began to craft a series of questions that would serve as an agenda for him to be able to enhance his own learnings.

As John meticulously framed these questions, he recognized their strategic significance. They weren't merely inquiries; they were keys to unlocking a deeper understanding of the practical dimensions of the Business Analyst realm. Little did he know that these questions would serve as a roadmap, guiding him through the complexities of his new responsibilities and paving the way for a fruitful collaboration with Process Peters and his team.

John's Meeting Agenda

What is the role of Process Peters?

Seeking clarity on the specific responsibilities and contributions that defined Process Peters' role as an SME.

What does Process Peters organizational structure look like?

Delving into the organizational structure to understand the hierarchical layout within which Process Peters operated.

Where does he (and his broader team) fit into the company structure?

Uncovering the positioning of Process Peters and his team within the broader organizational framework.

What are the functions performed by Process Peters and his team?

Exploring the day-to-day operations and functions carried out by Process Peters and his team.

> **What value add is John expected to bring to this team?**
>
> Clarifying the expectations regarding John's role and the unique contributions he was expected to make to Process Peters' team.

The 1ˢᵗ Real Meeting

John's nerves echoed through the quiet meeting room as he awaited the encounter that set this meeting apart from all the others he had attended. Seated at the table, he sifted through his notes, stealing glances at the clock ticking away. The anticipation hung in the air like an unspoken tension.

Five minutes before the scheduled time, John found himself in the room alone, amplifying the weight of the impending meeting. Sipping from his water bottle, he checked his watch once more, his eyes scanning the notes on his laptop screen. After a final review, he closed the lid, took a deep breath, and directed his gaze towards the door.

In the moments preceding the meeting, John attempted to visualize the person he was about to meet. Not in terms of physical appearance, but from a personality standpoint. He was determined to approach this encounter with a keen awareness of the individual behind the professional façade.

The door swung open, breaking the silence. A tall, middle-aged man entered, radiating a sense of assurance. Extending his hand towards John, he greeted him with a warm smile, "You must be the rookie they assigned to me?" Caught off guard, John's response was a mix of honesty and humor, "Yep! That's me. Hope you aren't too disappointed?"

Process Peters, with a concerned look, replied, "How can I be disappointed? We have just met. Although let's see how this meeting goes before I jump to any conclusions." These words added a layer of nervousness, but the friendly smile and comforting demeanor of Process Peters reassured John that he might have been overthinking.

As the meeting unfolded, Process Peters delved into a comprehensive overview of his roles and responsibilities, unraveling the core functions of his team and their position within the broader organization. John sat in slight disbelief as each topic he had prepared questions for was meticulously addressed by Process Peters.

To John's surprise, the conversation expanded beyond the anticipated queries. Process Peters navigated through the challenges his team faced, providing insights into major projects and deliverables over the past 12 months. He painted a vivid picture of the future roadmap for the financial year's remainder, emphasizing the need for additional team members due to the workload.

Frantically taking notes, John sensed Process Peters observing his efforts. With a smile, Process Peters interrupted, "You know, you can always ask me to slow down." John looked at him, an expression of disbelief and uncertainty on his face, silently questioning if he could truly interrupt this flow of information. Process Peters laughed, breaking the tension, and reassured him, "You are no longer in college, my friend. In the professional world, you are allowed the courtesy to interrupt people politely and ask them to slow down. This is about practical, hands-on learning. You won't be able to refer to your textbook or lecture notes later. So do whatever is required for YOU to better grasp what I am trying to explain."

The words resonated with John, marking a shift in mindset. He realized that this was not just a meeting—it was an opportunity for immersive learning, a chance to navigate the complexities of real-world business analysis. With a newfound sense of confidence, John continued to absorb the wealth of information laid out before him, recognizing that this mentorship would be a cornerstone in his journey towards becoming a proficient Business Analyst.

"I need to head off to my next meeting," announced Process Peters, glancing at his watch. John couldn't believe how quickly the hour had flown by. The conversation had been engaging, and the learning process was more extensive than he could have imagined. He found himself yearning for more insights.

As the realization dawned that the meeting was coming to an end, Process Peters inquired, "Do you have any questions for me?" The eagerness to continue learning prompted John to respond, "I just have two questions. Can I have another session with you? Also, what value am I expected to bring to the team to be deemed useful?"

Process Peters, seemingly impressed by the inquiries, replied, "My calendar is up to date, so please feel free to book any available time slot. As for your second question, the best value you can bring to the team would be your curiosity and your willingness to learn. Since you are a graduate, you will be allowed to make some mistakes—a luxury most of us don't have. So, learn as much as you want, make mistakes, improve, and, best of all, have fun doing it."

With a warm smile, Process Peters concluded, "And now, if you would excuse me, I need to rush to my next meeting. It was lovely meeting you, John Smith." With those words, he extended a handshake, and as swiftly as he had entered the room, Process Peters departed, leaving John with a sense of gratitude and a newfound enthusiasm for the journey ahead.

Organizational Structure

The weeks following that pivotal initial meeting with Process Peters were a whirlwind of excitement and continuous learning. John found himself immersed in a sea of new insights and knowledge, thanks to his ongoing meetings with Process Peters. These encounters extended beyond the one-on-one sessions, introducing John to the broader team within the department known as the Centre of Excellence.

The Centre of Excellence, as John discovered, played a crucial role in ensuring that key processes across all departments were not only up to date but also fit for purpose. Their guiding principle was one of continuous improvement, a mantra that echoed in every aspect of their work.

After two weeks of soaking in knowledge, John received his first official assignment. The task at hand involved documenting the changes in the organizational structure that had occurred over time. This seemingly straightforward task held paramount importance, not only to fulfill the assigned duty but also to accurately identify the relevant stakeholders for each department.

As John delved into the intricate details of the task, enthusiasm soon gave way to a sense of dreadful panic. The task, initially perceived as manageable, now revealed its complexity. The absence of clear documents outlining the organizational changes added an unexpected layer of challenge. It was a moment of realization for John, a reminder that in the world of practical application, tasks could prove to be more intricate than anticipated. The weeks ahead promised not just learning, but also the invaluable experience of navigating through the uncertainties and challenges that come with real-world business analysis.

In one of the meetings John had asked Process Peters a simple question. "Why do we need to review and understand the organization structure? What's the importance of this activity?".

Process Peters paused for a moment, considering John's question. It was a seemingly simple query that held profound implications for anyone stepping into the dynamic realm of business analysis. As he gathered his thoughts, Process Peters began to articulate the significance of reviewing and understanding the organization structure.

"John," he began, "reviewing and understanding the organization structure is like deciphering the blueprint of a complex machine. Let me break down the importance for you."

IMPORTANCE OF UNDERSTANDING THE ORGANISATION STRUCTURE

1. Alignment with Objectives:

"Firstly, it ensures that every individual, every department is aligned with the overall objectives of the organization. Like cogs in a machine, each part should work cohesively towards a common goal. Understanding the structure ensures everyone knows their role in achieving that goal."

2. Efficient Communication:

"Secondly, it facilitates efficient communication. By knowing the reporting relationships and how information flows, we can streamline communication channels. This is crucial for effective decision-making and problem-solving."

3. Identifying Stakeholders:

"When you understand the organization structure, you can accurately identify stakeholders. Knowing who plays a key role in decision-making and who is impacted by decisions helps us manage relationships and ensure that everyone who needs to be involved is included."

4. Adapting to Change:

"Organizations are dynamic, and structures may evolve. By regularly reviewing the structure, we can adapt to changes more seamlessly. This adaptability is vital in an ever-changing business landscape."

5. Resource Allocation:

"Understanding the organization structure aids in resource allocation. It helps us know where expertise lies, who to approach for specific tasks, and how to distribute resources efficiently."

6. Cultural Insights:

"The organization structure also provides insights into the organizational culture. The way information flows, how decisions are made, and the overall hierarchy all contribute to the culture. Understanding this helps us navigate the workplace more effectively."

As Process Peters concluded his explanation, he emphasized, "In essence, John, reviewing the organization structure is not just a procedural activity. It's a strategic necessity. It's about ensuring that every part of the organization is not just functioning but thriving in a synchronized manner. It's about empowering individuals with the knowledge of how they fit into the larger picture. It's a foundational step towards effective business analysis."

John, jotting down notes in his learning journal, couldn't help but appreciate the depth of insight that this seemingly simple question had unravelled. The importance of understanding the organization structure now echoed in his mind as a fundamental pillar in the journey of becoming a proficient Business Analyst.

Process Peters continued, "Now the big question is, how do I do it? I mean how would you go about understanding an organization structure? There are several ways of doing this, but here are some ways that have worked well for me in the past. I hope you can draw your own methods in future, but the once I am about to explain will get you started."

HOW TO UNDERSTAND AN ORGANISATIONAL STRUCTURE

1. Review Organizational Charts:

- Organizational charts visually represent the hierarchy of positions and reporting relationships within a company. Reviewing these charts provides a quick overview of key roles and departments.

2. Study Job Descriptions and Responsibilities:

- Job descriptions outline the responsibilities and requirements for each role within the organization. Studying these documents can provide insights into the functions of different positions.

3. Analyse Reporting Relationships:

- Understand the reporting relationships between positions. Identify who reports to whom, recognizing the hierarchy and the flow of authority.

4. Explore Departmental Functions:

- Examine the functions and responsibilities of each department. This helps you understand the specific roles each department plays in achieving the organization's goals.

5. Consider Communication Channels:

- Evaluate how communication flows within the organization. Recognize formal communication channels, such as official reports and meetings, as well as informal channels like team collaborations.

6. Assess Decision-Making Processes:

- Identify how decisions are made within the organization. Understand whether decisions are centralized, with authority resting at the top, or decentralized, allowing for more distributed decision-making.

7. Understand the Chain of Command:

- Clarify the chain of command by recognizing who holds decision-making authority at different levels. This helps you understand how strategic decisions are communicated and executed.

8. Look at the Size and Scope of Teams:

- Examine the size and scope of teams within the organization. Recognize whether teams are functional, cross-functional, or project-based, as this impacts how work is organized and executed.

9. Explore Cultural Aspects:

- Consider the organizational culture. Understand the values, norms, and communication styles prevalent in the organization, as these elements shape how people interact and work together.

10. Speak with Colleagues:

- Engage in conversations with colleagues to gain insights into the practical aspects of the organizational structure. Ask about their roles, reporting relationships, and how they collaborate with other teams.

11. Review Historical Changes:

- Investigate any historical changes in the organizational structure. Understanding past adjustments can provide context for the current state and potential future changes.

Armed with the insights shared by Process Peters, John embarked on the journey of unraveling the intricate tapestry of the organizational structure. Applying the techniques, he had learned, he found the task to be more structured and enjoyable than anticipated. One simple yet effective step he took was to engage with the Human Resources (HR) team of the company.

Understanding that HR teams typically hold detailed information about organizational structures, John reached out to them for assistance. As a rule of thumb, HR is tasked with maintaining and updating these details, making them a valuable resource for anyone navigating the complexities of an organization. When the HR team learned about John's mission and how it aligned with their responsibilities, they gladly offered their support, recognizing the mutual benefit.

This marked a significant milestone for John – his first business buy-in. The HR team's willingness to assist signified not only their cooperation but also a recognition of the shared value in maintaining a well-understood and accessible organizational structure. The collaborative spirit demonstrated in this interaction hinted at the importance of building alliances within different departments, a lesson John was quick to internalize.

With the support of the HR team, John's exploration into the organizational structure took on a more guided and purposeful trajectory. This early success fueled his confidence, reinforcing the notion that in the world of business analysis, effective collaboration and leveraging existing resources are pivotal to achieving meaningful outcomes.

BUSINESS BUY IN

Business buy-in refers to the acceptance, support, and approval of a business idea, initiative, or decision by key stakeholders within an organization. When there is business buy-in, individuals and teams are on board with the proposed action, understand its value, and commit to its success. This involves aligning goals, committing resources, active participation, and open communication to ensure the initiative's effective implementation and positive outcomes.

Stakeholder Analysis

After nearly ten weeks of dedicated effort, John successfully completed the organizational structure for the company, a significant feat given its 5000 employees and ongoing growth. His achievement was met with pride, not only from himself but also from the colleagues in the HR team who were impressed by the quality of his work.

In a noteworthy recognition, Process Peters singled out John by name in the last all-hands meeting, a moment that marked a significant milestone in his journey within the company. Gradually, John had transformed from being the new kid on the block to someone who was building a positive reputation. Fueled by his growing enthusiasm, he felt ready to tackle new and complex challenges.

However, just when everything seemed to be going well, John encountered a harsh reality check in the form of office politics—a formidable force that often lurks beneath the surface of workplace dynamics, presenting unexpected challenges and complexities. The stage was set for John to navigate this intricate landscape and learn valuable lessons about the nuanced aspects of corporate life.

Tasked with performing a stakeholder analysis for the latest project, John found himself at the intersection of organizational intricacies and a crucial customer experience initiative. The project aimed to review and validate the end-to-end customer journey for one of their best-selling products, with the goal of seamlessly replacing it while enhancing the overall customer experience.

Thanks to the comprehensive organizational structure review he had undertaken, John possessed a solid understanding of the various departments and teams that could potentially be impacted by this initiative. However, recognizing the need for additional guidance, he sought insights from Process Peters in a strategic move to set himself up for success.

In their next meeting, Process Peters emphasized the importance of engaging the Subject Matter Expert (SME) from the current products team. This SME would play a pivotal role in providing a comprehensive overview of the product itself, shedding light on the intricacies of the processes involved. Importantly, they could offer clarity on which departments were directly affected by these processes and identify key individuals within each department who could provide a detailed view of their processes specific to this particular product.

This guidance from Process Peters became a key directive for John's stakeholder analysis. It highlighted the significance of involving not only the broader departments but also those individuals deeply immersed in the day-to-day workings of the product in question. By understanding the processes from the ground up and identifying key stakeholders within each department, John would be better positioned to conduct a thorough analysis and ensure that the upcoming changes would be seamlessly integrated into the existing workflows.

Armed with this strategic direction, John was ready to embark on the stakeholder analysis with a focused approach, recognizing the importance of granular insights to make the project a success and ensure an enhanced customer experience with the new product.

John's initial enthusiasm and confidence was short lived. Facing a formidable challenge in navigating the complexities of the stakeholder landscape, John found himself in a particularly difficult situation with Product Pablo. With over 20 years of dedication to the company and an intimate understanding of the current best-selling product, Product Pablo was emotionally attached to his creation. The news of its replacement had left him anxious and angry, making it challenging for John to secure meaningful meetings or glean valuable insights from their interactions.

Despite persistent efforts over two weeks, John's progress had been minimal, and he felt the weight of potential judgment from Process Peters and his team. With Process Peters on a four-week leave and unable to offer guidance, John noticed a crucial piece of information in an out-of-office response. It mentioned reaching out to Process Peters' manager, Stakeholder Steve, in case of urgent matters.

Realizing the urgency of his situation, John wasted no time and promptly booked a meeting with Stakeholder Steve. This presented a fresh opportunity to seek guidance, share his challenges with Product Pablo, and discuss potential strategies to navigate the sensitive dynamics surrounding the replacement of the cherished best-selling product. As the meeting date approached, John hoped that engaging with Stakeholder Steve would provide the much-needed support and insights to overcome the roadblocks in his stakeholder analysis.

Stakeholder Steve, welcoming and supportive, had promptly accepted John's meeting invitation. His reassurance extended beyond a mere acknowledgment as he emailed John, extending an open invitation to his office for any assistance required in Process Peters' absence. This gesture provided a comforting backdrop for John, who felt supported and encouraged.

As the meeting unfolded, John candidly laid out the challenges he faced with Product Pablo and the hindrances in progressing with the stakeholder analysis. Stakeholder Steve, radiating a calm and confident demeanor, attentively absorbed the information. Once John had articulated the situation, Stakeholder Steve began to share his insights.

"John, you are a graduate, and the learning journey ahead of you is vast. What you're currently experiencing is not only typical human behavior but also an introduction to the taste of corporate office politics," Stakeholder Steve explained. John, eager to absorb wisdom, listened intently as Stakeholder Steve continued, "Let me shed some light on what office politics means."

Stakeholder Steve's willingness to provide guidance and his candid discussion about the nuances of office politics set the stage for John to gain valuable insights into the dynamics of corporate environments. As he delved into the explanation, Stakeholder Steve aimed to equip John with a deeper understanding of the factors at play and strategies to navigate the intricate landscape of office politics.

OFFICE POLITICS

Office politics refers to the activities, behaviors, and strategies employed by individuals within an organization to gain advantages, influence decisions, or achieve personal objectives. It involves the informal power struggles, alliances, and subtle maneuvering that take place in a workplace, often beyond the official organizational structure and policies.

Key Characteristics of Office Politics

Influence and Power Play:

Individuals engage in tactics to increase their influence and power within the organization. This may involve forming alliances, building relationships with influential figures, or strategically positioning oneself.

Navigating Relationships:

Office politics often centers around interpersonal relationships. It includes actions such as networking, forming alliances, or managing conflicts to enhance one's standing or achieve specific goals.

Decision-Making Dynamics:

Individuals may use office politics to influence decision-making processes. This can involve lobbying, presenting information strategically, or leveraging personal connections to shape outcomes in their favor.

Information Control:

Controlling information and its flow is a common aspect of office politics. Individuals may selectively share or withhold information to gain an advantage, manipulate perceptions, or protect their interests.

Strategic Communication:

Communication is a tool in office politics. People may employ strategic communication to convey messages that align with their objectives, whether it's building a positive image, discrediting others, or positioning themselves for opportunities.

Perception Management:

Managing how others perceive oneself is a key element. This includes creating a positive image, building a personal brand, or influencing the perception of one's contributions and capabilities.

Competition and Rivalry:

Office politics often involves competition and rivalry among colleagues. Individuals may vie for promotions, recognition, or resources, leading to tensions and rivalries within the workplace.

Informal Networks:

Informal networks, often based on personal relationships and shared interests, play a significant role. Being part of the right network can provide access to valuable information, opportunities, and support.

Stakeholder Steve continued, "While office politics is a natural aspect of any workplace, it becomes problematic when it hampers collaboration, creates a toxic work environment, or undermines organizational goals. Effectively navigating office politics requires a balance between achieving personal objectives and contributing positively to the overall success of the organization".

Absorbing Stakeholder Steve's wisdom, John's focus intensified as he recognized the significance of Information Control in the case of Product Pablo. The idea that withholding information might safeguard individual interests resonated, but Stakeholder Steve highlighted the potential missed opportunities for Product Pablo in the process. The solution, Stakeholder Steve suggested, lay in helping Product Pablo realize the broader possibilities that the new product could bring.

To initiate this process, Stakeholder Steve proposed a comprehensive stakeholder analysis. John was encouraged to delve into Product Pablo's organization structure and compile a list of individuals with stakes in both the old and new products. Recognizing that Product Patrick would spearhead the new product initiative, Stakeholder Steve advised exploring his organization structure as well.

Feverishly taking notes, John committed to this actionable plan. When he had captured all the key points, he looked up at Stakeholder Steve and sought approval for another meeting in the near future. "Is it okay if I set up another meeting with you in 2-3 days' time? I will have gathered all the information you've asked for by then," John proposed. Stakeholder Steve responded with a reassuring smile and a nod of agreement, setting the stage for the next phase of John's strategic approach to navigate the intricacies of the stakeholder landscape.

With a clear mission and a newfound understanding, John plunged headfirst into the tasks assigned by Stakeholder Steve. Empowered by the realization that the success of the project would not only impact him but also reflect on Stakeholder Steve and the broader team, John felt assured of their unwavering support. Much like Process Peters, Stakeholder Steve had demonstrated a commitment to providing the necessary guidance and backing for John to successfully deliver the project outcomes.

This assurance became a powerful confidence booster for John, evident in his overall mood and how he adeptly navigated through the assigned tasks. Realizing that he had a solid support system behind him fueled his determination to excel in the stakeholder analysis and contribute to the success of the project.

As the day of the second meeting with Stakeholder Steve approached, John found himself well-prepared. Armed with valuable insights, organizational structures, and stakeholder lists, he was ready to engage in a strategic discussion and seek further guidance to refine his approach. The journey that had initially seemed challenging now held the promise of growth and learning, thanks to the mentorship and support provided by Stakeholder Steve and the broader team.

Stakeholder Steve, thoroughly impressed by John's diligence and the quality of work produced, expressed his satisfaction with a warm acknowledgment. While there were a few corrections and adjustments to the stakeholder list, overall, Stakeholder Steve commended John for a job well done. "Well done, John! This is good work," he praised, causing John's face to light up with happiness.

"Now, do you understand the concept of RACI in project management?" Stakeholder Steve inquired. John nodded and responded, "Yes, I learned the concept during my university studies but have not practiced it in a practical sense."

"That's fine. As long as you know the basics, it will be easier for me to explain things to you. Although, we won't be touching on RACI today. Today, we do a simple stakeholder analysis or mapping," Stakeholder Steve clarified, setting the stage for the next phase of John's learning journey in navigating the complexities of project management and stakeholder dynamics.

STAKEHOLDER ANALYSIS

Stakeholder analysis is a systematic process used in project management to identify, understand, and assess the individuals, groups, or organizations that may be affected by or can affect a project. The purpose of stakeholder analysis is to gather information about stakeholders, their interests, influence, and potential impact on the project. This analysis helps project managers make informed decisions, manage expectations, and develop effective strategies for engaging and communicating with stakeholders throughout the project lifecycle.

Key Elements of Stakeholder Analysis

Identification:

Identifying all potential stakeholders involved in or affected by the project. This includes internal and external individuals, groups, or organizations.

Understanding Interests and Expectations:

Analyzing the interests, expectations, and concerns of each stakeholder. This involves understanding their perspectives, motivations, and the potential impact of the project on them.

Assessing Influence:

Evaluating the level of influence each stakeholder has on the project. Some stakeholders may have significant decision-making power or the ability to impact project outcomes.

Mapping Relationships:

Visualizing the relationships and interactions between different stakeholders. This helps in understanding potential conflicts, alliances, or dependencies.

Prioritization:

Prioritizing stakeholders based on their importance, influence, and potential impact. This helps in allocating resources and attention effectively.

Communication and Engagement Planning:

Developing strategies for communicating with and engaging stakeholders. This includes defining communication channels, messages, and methods for involving stakeholders in decision-making processes.

"So in summary", continued Stakeholder Steve, "stakeholder analysis is an ongoing process, and as the project evolves, the dynamics of stakeholder relationships may change. Regularly updating and revisiting the stakeholder analysis ensures that project managers stay informed and adapt their strategies to effectively manage stakeholder expectations and contribute to the project's success."

Stakeholder Steve, sensing the potential overwhelm in processing the wealth of information, offered a reassuring perspective. "I understand that this amount of information could be overwhelming at first," he acknowledged, "but remember the basics, and you will find your way back into the process if you ever feel lost or unsure." Emphasizing the practical aspect of the learning process, Stakeholder Steve introduced the concept of a simple stakeholder mapping exercise as a helpful tool for visual representation.

"While the definition and details are good for learning, a simple stakeholder mapping exercise often helps with a visual representation of your information," Stakeholder Steve continued. He introduced the idea of an axis diagram, a straightforward method for creating a visual representation. In this diagram, the Y-axis represents the Power and/or Influence of a stakeholder, while the X-axis represents the Interest or Impact of a particular individual, group, or team.

Stakeholder Steve decided to illustrate the concept with an example, aiming to provide John with a tangible and practical understanding of stakeholder mapping through visual representation.

Opening his laptop, Stakeholder Steve navigated through his files with purpose until he located the specific template he had in mind. Satisfied with his find, he seamlessly attached the template to an email that he carefully compiled for John. With a few clicks, Stakeholder Steve sent the email, effectively providing John with the visual representation template that would serve as a valuable tool in the stakeholder mapping exercise. This practical approach aimed to empower John with a hands-on tool to apply the concepts discussed and enhance his understanding of stakeholder analysis through visual representation.

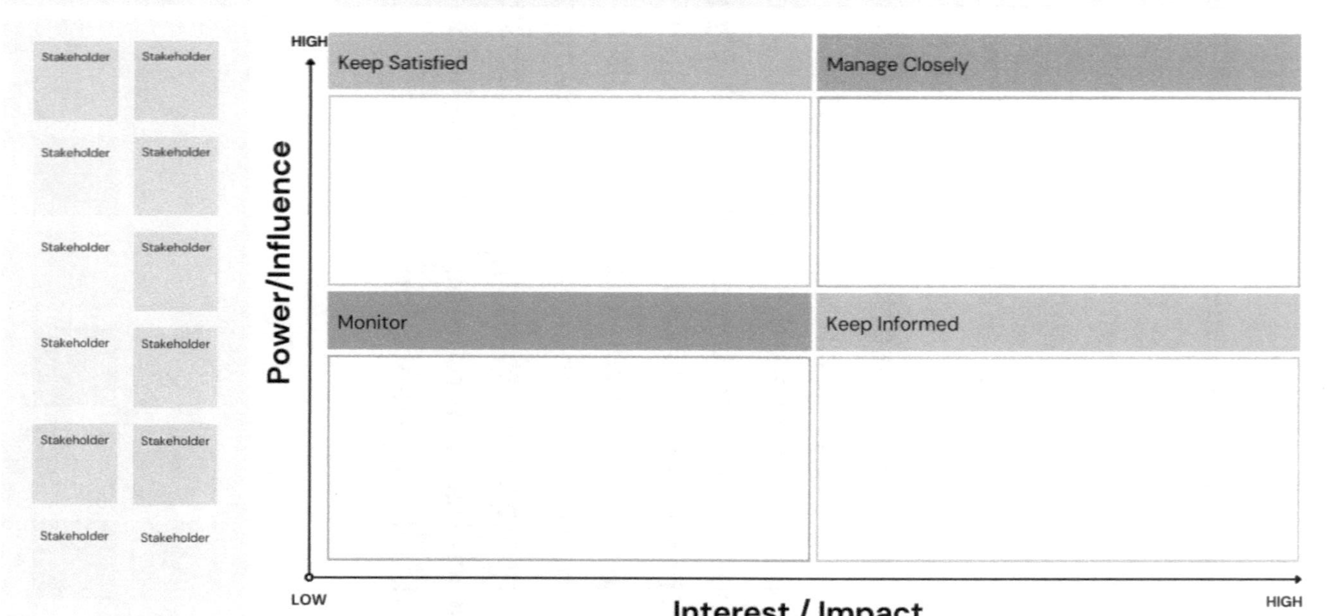

A Sample Template Of Stakeholder Mapping

As John opened the email and glimpsed the template, his jaw dropped in awe. The simplicity yet power of the visual representation struck him immediately. Overflowing with gratitude, he couldn't help but express his thanks to Stakeholder Steve. Immersed in the visual possibilities, John began mentally placing the names of the stakeholders he had collected into their respective columns, envisioning the structured clarity that the template provided.

Stakeholder Steve, observing John's reaction with admiration, explained, "This is usually a team exercise, you see. While you can populate most of it based on the details you have gathered, it is advisable and also good practice to actually gather these stakeholders into a meeting and ask them to nominate themselves a column in the map. It saves you a lot of heartache later." He continued, offering a strategic suggestion, "Although given the complex nature and the type of people involved, I suggest you wait for Process Peters to return from leave, and let him lead that part. You can always shadow and learn from him while he leads the meeting."

With these final words of wisdom, Stakeholder Steve excused himself from the meeting, leaving John amazed at how quickly and efficiently things had transformed from feeling helpless to being very much in control. John discovered that the collaborative efforts of a supportive team, coupled with strategic methodologies, could turn seemingly overwhelming challenges into manageable and rewarding endeavors.

---- ✦✦ ----

With the right guidance, techniques, and tools, tackling large and complex tasks could be approached with relative ease.

– Anupamm Singh

---- ✦✦ ----

As Process Peters returned from his leave, a cloud of stress hung over him regarding the status of the project. Uncertain about what might have transpired in his absence and how John coped during that time, he quickly skimmed through his emails. Determined to get a firsthand account, he made his way to John's desk and, upon finding him, suggested they grab a coffee to discuss the activities undertaken in his absence.

John felt a mixture of excitement and apprehension as he followed Process Peters to the elevator. The soft ding of the arriving lift broke the silence, and they stepped in, joined by a few other employees. As the doors closed, Process Peters turned to John with a smile.

"So, John, how have things been while I was away?" he asked, his tone casual.

John smiled back, "It was quite an experience, Process Peters. I've been deeply involved with the project, and I'm eager to update you."

The elevator descended smoothly. John, curious about his mentor's vacation, asked, "How was your holiday? Where did you go?"

Process Peters' face brightened as he reminisced. "I went to Bali. It was amazing—the beaches, the culture, everything was just perfect."

John's eyes lit up with interest. "That sounds incredible! I've always wanted to visit Bali. What did you do there?"

"Oh, I did so much. I explored several temples, went snorkeling in crystal-clear waters, and even took a cooking class to learn some local recipes. The weather was fantastic—sunny and warm, perfect for exploring," Process Peters replied, clearly enjoying sharing his experiences.

"Wow, that sounds like a dream vacation," John replied enthusiastically. "How was the food?"

"The food was amazing," Process Peters said. "Fresh seafood, exotic fruits, and a lot of spicy dishes. I even brought back some spices to try and recreate the recipes at home."

As the elevator reached the ground floor, they exited and walked towards the coffee shop. The aroma of freshly brewed coffee greeted them as they entered. The barista, a cheerful young woman, smiled and greeted them.

Process Peters glanced at the menu, then turned to John. "What will you have, John? My treat."

"I'll have a latte, thank you," John replied.

"One latte and one flat white, please," Process Peters ordered.

As they waited for their coffees, Process Peters continued, "It's always a bit of a shock coming back to the office after a relaxing vacation. The first day back is usually the toughest—catching up on emails, meetings, and getting back into the groove."

John nodded in understanding. "I can imagine. It's good to have you back, though. The team missed you."

Their coffee arrived, and they took a seat in a quiet corner of the coffee shop. Process Peters took a sip of his flat white, savoring the rich flavor. "So, tell me, John, how did you find handling the project on your own?"

John took a deep breath and began, "It was quite an experience, Process Peters. Initially, I struggled to get much support from Product Pablo. He's very protective of his creation, and the thought of replacing the legacy product didn't sit well with him. Every time I tried to set up a meeting, he would avoid my requests, always pretending to be busy."

Process Peters nodded, understanding the challenge. "Product Pablo can be difficult when it comes to his work. How did you manage to navigate that?"

"Stakeholder Steve was a huge help," John continued. "After repeatedly failing to get through to Product Pablo, I reached out to Stakeholder Steve. He advised me to change my approach and focus on building trust. Stakeholder Steve explained the importance of empathy and understanding Product Pablo's perspective. He mentored me on how to perform a thorough stakeholder analysis, which included mapping out the key players and understanding their interests and concerns."

John took a sip of his latte, then went on. "Following Stakeholder Steve's advice, I decided to try a more personal touch. Instead of formal meetings, I invited both Product Pablo and Product Patrick for coffee. I thought a casual setup might help ease the tension and encourage open communication. To my relief, they both agreed."

Process Peters leaned in, clearly interested. "That's a smart move. How did it go?"

John smiled, recalling the moment. "The meeting started a bit awkwardly, but as we settled in, the atmosphere became more relaxed. Over coffee, we discussed the project in a more informal setting. I let Product Pablo talk about his work and listened attentively. I assured him that the goal was not to discard his efforts but to build on them and create something even better."

He continued, "Product Patrick was supportive and helped bridge the gap. He emphasized the need for innovation while respecting Product Pablo's contributions. At first, the conversation was tentative, with Product Pablo clearly wary of the changes being proposed. However, Product Patrick's diplomatic approach helped ease the tension. He acknowledged Product Pablo's hard work and the significance of the legacy product to the company's success.

Product Patrick said, 'Product Pablo, your product has been a cornerstone for our team. It's because of the solid foundation you've built that we can even think about innovating further. We aren't trying to replace your work; we're looking to enhance it and ensure it stays relevant in the future.'

Product Pablo seemed to soften at these words, and I could see the shift in his demeanor. Product Patrick then shared some insights into the market trends and how the new version could address emerging customer needs more effectively. He painted a picture of a future where Product Pablo's legacy would continue to thrive, albeit in a more advanced form.

As the discussion progressed, Product Patrick took the opportunity to present some preliminary ideas on how we could transition from the old product to the new one. He highlighted the features that would be retained and how the core essence of Product Pablo's creation would remain intact. He also explained how we planned to document the process meticulously, ensuring that Product Pablo's expertise and insights were preserved.

Product Patrick added, 'This isn't just a project for us, Product Pablo. It's a way to honor your contribution and build upon it. We need your guidance to make sure we do it right.'

By the end of the meeting, Product Pablo was more open to the idea and agreed to provide the information I needed. We managed to iron out some sensitive issues, such as data migration challenges and potential disruptions to existing users. Product Pablo's input was invaluable here; his deep understanding of the product's architecture helped us identify potential pitfalls and develop strategies to mitigate them.

One particularly sensitive issue was the transition period for existing users. Product Pablo was concerned about their experience and potential backlash if things didn't go smoothly. We discussed creating a detailed communication plan to keep users informed and supported throughout the transition. Product Pablo suggested setting up a dedicated support team to handle any issues that might arise, which we all agreed was a great idea.

Product Patrick and I assured Product Pablo that his legacy would not only be preserved but would also be celebrated as the foundation for the next generation of our product. This was a turning point for the project. Product Pablo's initial resistance had transformed into cautious optimism, and he was now willing to actively participate in the transition process.

As we wrapped up, Product Pablo remarked, 'I still have my reservations, but I can see the potential benefits. I appreciate that you're involving me in the process. Let's make sure we get it right.'

I felt a sense of accomplishment as we left the coffee shop. The meeting had not only resolved some immediate concerns but had also set a collaborative tone for the rest of the project. With Product Pablo on board, we had the expertise and support needed to move forward confidently.

John paused, taking a moment to reflect. 'That meeting was a turning point, Process Peters. It showed me the power of empathy and open communication in overcoming resistance and building strong stakeholder relationships.'

"Well done, John! You have exceeded my expectations in many ways," exclaimed Process Peters, his admiration evident in both his tone and expression. John felt a swell of pride and relief wash over him. The weeks of hard work, late nights, and challenging conversations had paid off.

Process Peters leaned forward, his eyes reflecting genuine appreciation. "Feeling confident in your capabilities, I believe it's time to take things to the next level. Given that you are almost at the end of your secondment term, I think it's appropriate to start discussing your future within the company."

John's heart raced with anticipation. This was the moment he had been working toward, a validation of his efforts and a stepping stone to greater opportunities. Process Peters continued, "You have proven yourself enough through your diligent work, your ability to handle complex situations, and your exceptional stakeholder management skills. The way you managed to bring

Product Pablo on board, addressing his concerns while maintaining the integrity of the project, was particularly impressive."

Process Peters paused, giving John a moment to absorb the praise before continuing, "Once the stakeholder analysis component is complete, I will sit down with you to determine the next course of action for your career progression. I see great potential in you, and it's time to map out a path that will allow you to grow and contribute even more significantly to our projects."

John nodded, a mixture of excitement and gratitude filling him. "Thank you, Process Peters. I appreciate your confidence in me. I'm eager to complete the stakeholder analysis and discuss how I can continue to grow within the company."

Process Peters smiled, "Excellent. I have some thoughts about potential roles and projects that could benefit from your skills. For now, focus on wrapping up the stakeholder analysis. Ensure it's thorough and comprehensive, as this will be crucial for the project's success and a testament to your capabilities."

John felt invigorated, ready to tackle the final stages of the stakeholder analysis with renewed energy. The acknowledgment of his hard work and the prospect of future opportunities filled him with a sense of purpose.

Process Peters stood up, extending his hand. "I'm looking forward to our next discussion, John. Keep up the great work."

John shook his hand firmly, "Thank you, Process Peters. I won't let you down."

With these promising words, the duo departed from the coffee shop. John, filled with a sense of accomplishment and pride, walked back towards his desk, eagerly anticipating the next chapter in his career journey.

Chapter 03

Baptised By Process

Over the coming days, Process Peters showcased his expertise in running stakeholder meetings, leaving no doubt about his proficiency. This was especially evident in the pivotal meeting involving nearly 30 stakeholders—a diverse group comprising senior executives, department heads, project managers, and key team members. The room buzzed with anticipation as everyone gathered, aware of the meeting's importance for the project's success.

Process Peters started the meeting with a confident and welcoming introduction, setting a collaborative tone. He then seamlessly transitioned into a comprehensive presentation of the business plan. Using clear, precise language, he articulated the vision and strategic objectives of the new product, emphasizing its benefits and how it built upon the legacy product's strengths. His presentation was supported by well-designed slides that visually mapped out the key points, making complex information easily digestible.

As he spoke, John observed Process Peters' mastery in engaging the audience. He didn't just present the plan; he made sure to address the concerns and interests of various stakeholders, drawing them into the conversation. He posed thoughtful questions, inviting input and encouraging dialogue. This interactive approach ensured that everyone felt their voices were heard and valued.

When it came time to secure buy-in from key stakeholders, Process Peters employed a strategic approach. He had already identified the key influencers within the group and had tailored his arguments to resonate with their priorities. For the finance team, he highlighted cost efficiencies and projected ROI. For the marketing department, he focused on the enhanced features that would appeal to customers and drive sales. For the operations team, he detailed the streamlined processes that would improve efficiency and reduce downtime.

Throughout the session, Process Peters was adept at handling questions and addressing concerns. He anticipated potential objections and had prepared robust responses, backed by data and case studies. His calm and composed demeanor instilled confidence, and his thorough knowledge of the project was evident in every answer he provided.

One of the key moments was when he introduced the stakeholder map. With the aid of a large, interactive display, Process Peters demonstrated how each stakeholder fit into the broader picture. He used color-coded blocks to represent different departments and roles, and as he placed each stakeholder within their respective blocks, he explained their roles and responsibilities. This visual representation made it clear how everyone's contributions were interconnected and essential for the project's success.

The meeting wasn't just a top-down dissemination of information; it was a collaborative effort. Process Peters skillfully facilitated discussions, allowing stakeholders to express their thoughts and suggestions. He encouraged constructive feedback and was open to making adjustments based on the collective input. This approach not only secured buy-in but also fostered a sense of ownership and commitment among the stakeholders.

By the end of the meeting, there was a palpable sense of agreement and alignment. Process Peters had successfully navigated through the complexities of stakeholder dynamics, ensuring that everyone was on the same page. He wrapped up the session by summarizing the key decisions made and outlining the next steps, making sure that everyone was clear on their roles and responsibilities moving forward.

John, who had been taking diligent notes throughout, was deeply impressed by the way Process Peters had conducted the meeting. He had turned a potentially challenging session into a productive and collaborative experience. John saw firsthand how effective stakeholder management could drive a project forward, creating a unified vision and ensuring that everyone was invested in its success.

As the stakeholders dispersed, many of them approached Process Peters to express their appreciation and share their enthusiasm for the project. It was clear that his adept handling of the session had not only secured their buy-in but had also energized them for the work ahead.

John felt inspired and motivated by the experience. He realized that this was the level of expertise and finesse he aspired to achieve. Watching Process Peters in action had provided him with valuable insights and practical lessons on stakeholder engagement and project leadership. He was eager to apply these learnings to his own work and continue growing in his role.

The meeting was a testament to Process Peters' exceptional skills and strategic thinking. It had set a strong foundation for the project's success and had demonstrated the power of effective stakeholder management in achieving business goals. John knew that with mentors like Process Peters, his journey in the company was just beginning, and the future was filled with exciting possibilities.

Post-meeting, Process Peters ensured that a comprehensive summary and detailed meeting minutes were promptly sent to all attendees. The email, which landed in everyone's inbox within a few hours of the meeting's conclusion, was meticulously crafted. It began with a concise yet thorough recap of the discussions, highlighting the key points and decisions made during the session.

The summary included a clear outline of the business plan presented, the strategic objectives discussed, and the benefits of the new product. It also detailed the concerns raised by various stakeholders and the corresponding responses provided. This ensured that everyone, whether they had been vocal during the meeting or not, had a clear understanding of what was covered.

Attached to the email were the detailed meeting minutes, which provided a blow-by-blow account of the proceedings. Every significant comment, question, and answer was documented, along with the action items assigned to specific individuals. This level of detail was crucial for maintaining transparency and ensuring that no critical point was overlooked.

Process Peters made it a point to grant all attendees a week to review the documentation. This was not just a formality but a strategic move to foster inclusiveness and transparency. He encouraged the stakeholders to provide feedback or suggest changes if they felt that any part of the meeting had been misrepresented or if they had additional insights to offer.

In the email, Process Peters wrote, "Dear all, please find attached the summary and detailed minutes of our recent stakeholder meeting. I encourage you to review these documents thoroughly and share any feedback or suggestions for changes within the next week. Your input is invaluable in ensuring that our stakeholder analysis is comprehensive and accurate. Thank you for your active participation and continued support."

This gesture was well-received by the stakeholders. It demonstrated that their voices were not only heard but also respected and valued. It was a clear indication that Process Peters was committed to a collaborative approach, where every stakeholder's perspective was considered crucial for the project's success.

As the week progressed, several stakeholders responded with their feedback. Some provided minor corrections to the details, while others offered additional insights that had not been fully explored during the meeting. One senior executive pointed out a potential risk that needed further mitigation, while a project manager suggested a few additional stakeholders who should be involved in the next phase of the project.

Process Peters and John reviewed all the feedback meticulously. They updated the meeting minutes and summary documents accordingly, ensuring that every valid point was incorporated. This iterative process not only improved the accuracy of the stakeholder analysis but also reinforced the stakeholders' trust in the project leadership.

The updated documents were then redistributed to all attendees, along with a note from Process Peters acknowledging the contributions and summarizing the key changes made based on the feedback received. He also outlined the next steps, including the timeline for the upcoming stakeholder mapping exercise and the subsequent project milestones.

John was deeply impressed by Process Peters' commitment to thoroughness and inclusiveness. He realized that this process was not just about completing a task but about building a strong foundation of trust and collaboration. The transparency with which Process Peters operated ensured that everyone felt invested in the project's success.

The feedback loop also highlighted the dynamic nature of stakeholder management. It was a continuous process of communication, adjustment, and alignment, aimed at keeping everyone on the same page and addressing concerns proactively. John learned that this approach was vital for navigating the complexities of large projects and ensuring smooth progress.

As they moved forward with the project, John felt more confident and prepared. The experience of working closely with Process Peters had been incredibly educational, providing him with practical skills and insights that would be invaluable in his career. He was eager to apply these lessons to future projects and continue growing as a business analyst.

The meticulous follow-up post-meeting had solidified the stakeholders' commitment and set the stage for the successful execution of the project. It was a testament to the power of effective stakeholder management and the importance of transparency and collaboration in achieving business objectives.

Over the course of nearly three weeks, characterized by intense effort and numerous negotiation sessions, the stakeholder analysis was meticulously reviewed, refined, and ultimately signed off. Each day was filled with back-to-back meetings, collaborative workshops, and detailed discussions aimed at addressing every stakeholder's concerns and ensuring that their input was accurately reflected.

John, under the guidance of Process Peters, worked tirelessly to incorporate the feedback received from the initial review. The days often stretched into long hours, with John and the team delving into the particulars of the analysis. They scrutinized every detail, ensuring that the interests and influence of each stakeholder were correctly mapped and that all potential risks were identified and mitigated.

The negotiation sessions were particularly challenging. Stakeholders from various departments had different priorities and perspectives, often leading to intense discussions. Product Pablo, for instance, was initially reluctant to accept some of the proposed changes, fearing they might undermine the integrity of the legacy product. However, through patient negotiation and clear communication, John and Process Peters managed to reassure him that his concerns would be addressed, and his contributions valued.

Stakeholder Steve played a pivotal role during these sessions. His experience and diplomatic skills helped bridge gaps between differing viewpoints. He often stepped in to mediate when discussions became heated, ensuring that the focus remained on finding collaborative solutions rather than letting disagreements stall progress.

John observed and learned from these interactions, gaining valuable insights into the art of negotiation and stakeholder management. He saw firsthand how Process Peters navigated complex dynamics, balancing assertiveness with empathy to achieve consensus. This period of intense collaboration was an invaluable learning experience for John, enhancing his understanding of the subtleties involved in managing stakeholder relationships.

By the end of the three weeks, the stakeholder analysis had evolved into a comprehensive and cohesive document. It detailed not only the roles and influence of each stakeholder but also provided a strategic framework for ongoing engagement. The final version was a testament to the collective effort and dedication of the team.

The sign-off meeting was a significant milestone. Process Peters opened the session by acknowledging the hard work and contributions of everyone involved. He presented the refined stakeholder analysis, highlighting the key changes and improvements made based on the feedback received. The atmosphere in the room was one of cautious optimism as stakeholders reviewed the final document.

After a thorough review, there was a moment of collective agreement. One by one, stakeholders signaled their approval, some with nods and others with verbal affirmations. The sign-off was not just a formality; it was a symbol of unified commitment to the project's success. The stakeholder analysis had laid a strong foundation for the work ahead, ensuring that everyone was aligned and prepared to move forward.

With this crucial step completed, the stage was set for the next phase—the process review. This phase would involve a detailed examination of the existing workflows and procedures, identifying areas for improvement and developing strategies for seamless integration of the new product.

The process review signaled the beginning of a critical juncture in the project's progression. It was a phase that would require meticulous planning, innovative thinking, and robust execution. The success of this phase would determine how effectively the new product could be implemented and how smoothly the transition from the legacy system would be managed.

John felt a mix of excitement and responsibility as they embarked on this next phase. The successful completion of the stakeholder analysis had boosted his confidence, but he was acutely aware of the challenges that lay ahead. He was determined to apply the lessons he had learned and contribute to the process review with the same level of dedication and diligence.

As the team reconvened to plan the process review, John found himself more involved in strategic discussions. Process Peters entrusted him with significant responsibilities, reflecting his growing confidence in John's abilities. John's journey from a fresh graduate to a key player in the project was unfolding, marked by continuous learning and increasing contributions.

The process review would be a defining phase for the project, setting the course for its successful implementation. With the stakeholder analysis signed off and a unified team ready to tackle the challenges, John felt optimistic about the future.

The Performance Review

The week following the sign-off meeting, John found himself back in the rhythm of daily tasks and ongoing project activities. The successful completion of the stakeholder analysis had given him a renewed sense of purpose, and he was eager to tackle the next phase of the project. As he sifted through his morning emails, a particular subject line caught his eye: "Mid-Year Performance Review."

The sender was Process Peters. John felt a mixture of anticipation and curiosity as he opened the email. It read:

"Dear John,

I hope this message finds you well. As we approach the midpoint of the year, it is time for your Mid-Year Performance Review. This is an excellent opportunity to discuss your progress, achievements, and areas for further development. Your contributions to the recent stakeholder analysis have not gone unnoticed, and I look forward to our discussion.

Please find the attached document for you to complete before our meeting, outlining your self-assessment and goals for the next six months.

Meeting Details:

Date: [Upcoming Monday]

Time: 10:00 AM

Location: Conference Room B

Best regards,

Process Peters"

As he finished reading the email, John found himself unable to shake off the thoughts about the statement made by Process Peters during their coffee catch-up, regarding the next course of his career progression. Several weeks had passed since that conversation, and the absence of further discussions or updates had led John to forget the conversation. Now, with the Mid-Year Performance Review meeting on the horizon, those words resurfaced with a new sense of urgency and curiosity. As he mulled over various possibilities, questions raced through his mind.

"Does career progression mean I won't be a graduate Business Analyst anymore?" John wondered aloud. Reflecting on his current role within the Center of Excellence team, he contemplated, "I handle organization structure reviews and stakeholder analysis, but I haven't been involved in other initiatives like process reviews or data-related activities that the broader team works on. Does this suggest a potential shift in my responsibilities?"

John's mind buzzed with possibilities. He had seen colleagues transition from junior roles to more specialized positions, taking on projects that required deep expertise in areas like data analytics, process improvement, and strategic planning. He wondered if a similar path lay ahead for him.

John downloaded the attached document, which outlined the key areas for self-assessment: accomplishments, challenges faced, skills developed, and goals for the upcoming months. He reflected on his journey since joining the company—how much he had learned, the challenges he had overcome, and the milestones he had achieved.

Over the next few days, John diligently filled out the self-assessment. He detailed his work on the stakeholder analysis, emphasizing how he had managed to build trust and secure buy-in from key stakeholders like Product Pablo and Product Patrick. He highlighted the skills he had developed, particularly in stakeholder management, negotiation, and project planning. He also set ambitious yet achievable goals for the next six months, including taking on more leadership roles in upcoming projects and further enhancing his technical and analytical skills.

When the day of the meeting arrived, John dressed a bit more formally than usual, feeling the significance of the occasion. He arrived at Conference Room B a few minutes early, using the time to review his self-assessment one last time.

Entering the meeting room for his very first performance review, John couldn't shake off the nervous anticipation brought on by the meeting's title. Six months into his post-graduation role, he found himself in uncharted territory, unsure of what to expect from this formal process. He had prepared meticulously, reflecting on his achievements and challenges, but the uncertainty of what lay ahead made his heart race.

As he waited, John couldn't help but fidget with the edges of his notes. The minutes seemed to stretch into hours, each tick of the clock amplifying his anxiety. The door creaked open, and Process Peters walked in with a serious expression, accompanied by an unfamiliar face – HR Helen. John's anxiety escalated as he tried to decipher the significance of her presence.

A mix of thoughts flooded his mind. "Am I in trouble?" he wondered, his heart pounding in his chest. Process Peters greeted him with a firm handshake, a subtle smile playing on his lips, and introduced HR Helen. "John, this is Helen from HR. She'll be joining us for the review."

John, maintaining composure, exchanged pleasantries with HR Helen and took his seat. Despite their polite smiles, the gravity of the moment weighed heavily on him.

Process Peters, noting John's nervous demeanor, decided to lighten the mood. He teased, "You seem nervous, John. Wondering why I'm here with HR Helen?"

John managed a nervous chuckle, nodding in agreement. Process Peters continued with a deadpan expression, "Well, you are in a lot of trouble, of course."

The room's atmosphere became charged with mixed emotions. John's heart raced even faster, anxiety amplifying as a rush of thoughts swirled in his mind. He felt a lump form in his throat, and his palms began to sweat. Just as he was about to speak, HR Helen burst into laughter, setting off Process Peters into a fit of laughter as well, leaving John bewildered.

Before the confusion could fully settle, Process Peters, still chuckling, reassured John, "Relax, John. We're just having fun and pulling your leg. You're not in any trouble. On the contrary, HR Helen is here to explain your new role and the benefits that come with it, marking the official end of your probationary period. Since this is an official company process, I am required to have a representative from Human Resources with me to answer any questions you may have as accurately as possible."

The room's tension eased as John absorbed the unexpected turn of events. Relief washed over him, and he couldn't help but smile at the playful trick Process Peters had pulled. He straightened in his chair, eager to hear more about this new development.

HR Helen joined the conversation with a warm greeting, "Hello, John! First and foremost, congratulations on successfully completing your six-month probationary period with flying colors. We've heard nothing but good things about your work, and I can attest that the excellent job you did on the Organization Structure review significantly benefited my department."

John felt a sense of pride and accomplishment at her words, but he also knew there was more to come. HR Helen continued, her tone appreciative and encouraging. "Process Peters and I spent the past week meticulously reviewing your overall performance, assessing your core skills and deliverables, and evaluating your ability to work unsupervised. We hire around 50 graduates each year, and many struggle with the challenges of their initial tasks, often ending up with mundane and repetitive assignments. However, there are exceptional individuals, like yourself, who excel in many aspects, navigating complexities and challenges with tact and grit."

She paused to let her words sink in, then proceeded, "John, your ability to handle significant responsibilities from the get-go has been remarkable. The stakeholder analysis you led, the intricate negotiations you managed, and the proactive approach you took in addressing key challenges have set you apart. Your performance on the Organization Structure review was particularly impactful, providing invaluable insights that have already begun to shape our strategic planning."

John nodded, grateful for the acknowledgment. He had put his heart and soul into his work, often going beyond the call of duty to ensure everything was perfect.

HR Helen continued, "Our review highlighted several key strengths that you possess. Firstly, your analytical skills are outstanding. You have a keen ability to dissect complex problems and present clear, actionable solutions. Secondly, your communication and interpersonal skills have been exemplary. You've shown an innate ability to build rapport with stakeholders and work collaboratively to achieve common goals."

John felt his confidence growing with each positive comment. HR Helen's detailed feedback was not just a recognition of his hard work but also a testament to his potential.

"Furthermore," she said, "your ability to work independently has been commendable. While many new hires often require constant guidance and oversight, you have demonstrated the capacity to take initiative and drive projects forward with minimal supervision. This level of autonomy is something we highly value, as it indicates your readiness for more significant responsibilities."

Process Peters nodded in agreement, adding, "John, your proactive approach and willingness to learn have been key to your success. You've embraced every challenge with determination, and your contributions have had a tangible impact on our team's success."

HR Helen smiled and handed John an official letter, detailing the terms of his new permanent position. "With these exceptional qualities in mind, we are thrilled to offer you a permanent position as a Business Analyst. This role will come with increased responsibilities, reflecting your capabilities and the trust we place in you. You'll be involved in more strategic projects, including process reviews and data-related initiatives that align with your expressed interests and career goals."

John took the letter with a mixture of excitement and gratitude. As he skimmed through the details, he noted the significant salary increase and the comprehensive benefits package. It was clear that the company was investing in his future, and the acknowledgment of his hard work was incredibly rewarding.

"Moreover," HR Helen continued, "we want to support your professional growth. You will have access to various training programs and courses to further develop your skills. Additionally, we are looking to involve you in more strategic projects where you can continue to learn and make significant contributions."

Process Peters leaned forward, his tone sincere. "John, this is just the beginning. We believe in your potential, and we're committed to helping you achieve your career goals. Your new role will come with more responsibilities, and we trust that you will continue to excel. We're excited to see how you will grow and contribute even more to our team."

John felt a profound sense of accomplishment and anticipation for the future. The past six months had been challenging, but they had also been filled with opportunities for growth and learning. He was grateful for the support and mentorship he had received and looked forward to continuing his journey with the company.

"Thank you, HR Helen, and thank you, Process Peters," John said, his voice filled with emotion. "I am truly honored by this opportunity, and I am committed to continuing to work hard and contribute to our team's success."

"Now, let's move on to the most important topic for this meeting," said Process Peters. "What does all this mean for you in terms of next steps? Do you have an idea, John, as to what you would like to do next?" John shrugged his shoulders, implying that he doesn't have a clear plan. However, he added, "Well, I have been monitoring my colleagues, and I can see there are several options I can explore. The most logical one seems to be Process Analysis."

"Why would you think that?" asked Process Peters. John replied, "For starters, processes are crucial for almost everything. They help us understand the steps required to achieve a particular outcome." Process Peters was pleased with this response and said, "But you have some doubts?" John nodded in agreement. "Then ask away," said Process Peters, encouraging John to seek clarification on any uncertainties he may have.

Encouraged by the support, John asked his first question, "My current role is of a Graduate Business Analyst. If I choose the process path, what would or could be my official title?" "A good question," said Process Peters. "Since you have just come out of probation and technically you are still very new to the organization, the official title would be Business

Process Analyst." John nodded in acknowledgment. "And what are the typical skills required for this kind of role?" continued John with his line of questioning. To which Process Peters looked at HR Helen, and she pulled out a piece of paper from within her pile of paperwork. John looked at the paper. The title read, "Business Process Analyst Role Information." John read along.

Business Process Analyst Role Information

A Business Process Analyst is a professional who assists an organization improve their operations by analyzing, designing, and implementing more efficient and effective business processes. They are problem-solvers, communicators, and change agents who play a crucial role in enhancing the overall performance of an organization.

Skills and Qualities:

- ***Analytical Skills:*** Business Process Analysts should be able to identify patterns, trends, and areas for improvement within processes.

- ***Problem-Solving Skills:*** They need to devise creative and practical solutions to address process inefficiencies.

- ***Communication Skills:*** Clear and effective communication is essential for collaborating with different stakeholders and presenting findings and recommendations.

- ***Technical Proficiency:*** Familiarity with process modeling and automation tools can be advantageous.

- ***Attention to Detail:*** Accuracy in process documentation and analysis is critical to the success of their work.

- ***Change Management Skills:*** They need to help employees adapt to process changes and mitigate resistance.

- ***Knowledge of Industry and Business:*** Understanding the specific industry and business domain in which they work is important for providing relevant insights and solutions.

Role and Responsibilities:

- ***Process Assessment:*** Business Process Analysts assist in evaluating existing business processes within an organization. They document and understand how these processes work, including the steps involved, the people or departments responsible, and the technologies or tools used.

- ***Process Analysis:*** Once the processes are documented, Business Process Analysts analyze them to identify bottlenecks, inefficiencies, and areas where improvements are needed. This may involve gathering data, conducting interviews, and using analytical tools to assess process performance.

- ***Process Improvement:*** After identifying areas for improvement, Business Process Analysts assist with designing and implementing solutions. They collaborate with various stakeholders, including employees, managers, and technology teams, to create more efficient and effective processes. This can involve process redesign, automation, and the introduction of new technologies.

- ***Documentation:*** Business Process Analysts create detailed process documentation, including flowcharts, diagrams, and written procedures, to ensure that all stakeholders understand the new processes and can follow them consistently.

- ***Change Management:*** Implementing process improvements often requires change management to ensure that employees adapt to the new procedures smoothly. Business Process Analysts may assist in developing change management plans and providing support to employees during the transition.

- ***Monitoring and Evaluation:*** After implementing process improvements, Business Process Analysts continue to monitor and evaluate the performance of the updated processes. They collect data and feedback to assess the impact of the changes and make further refinements as necessary.

- ***Technology Integration:*** In many cases, Business Process Analysts work with IT departments to integrate technology solutions that can streamline processes, such as workflow management systems or process automation software.

- ***Communication:*** Effective communication is a crucial part of their role. They need to collaborate with various teams and departments, facilitate discussions, and present their findings and recommendations to management and stakeholders.

As John read through the document, HR Helen and Process Peters waited in silence. This was an important decision and they didn't want John to rush through. They wanted him to make an informed decision. Once John finished reading the document, he passed it to HR Helen, took a deep breadth and said "Most of the details resonate with me and I am quite confident in my abilities to be able to perform the role. However, I am not very sure about the data part."

Process Peters nodded appreciatively at John's thoughtful consideration. He then addressed John's concern about the data aspect of the role. "John, the data part is a skill that can be developed and refined over time. You don't need to be an expert from day one. We understand that as a Business Process Analyst, you might not have extensive experience in handling complex data sets. However, we provide training and support to help you build these skills gradually. It's about the willingness to learn and the commitment to improvement."

HR Helen chimed in, "John, we value your analytical skills and problem-solving abilities. These are strong foundations for diving into the data side of process analysis. Additionally, you'll have opportunities to collaborate with our data specialists and learn from their expertise. Consider it as a growth opportunity, and we'll provide the necessary resources for your development."

John nodded, absorbing the information. It seemed like a challenge worth taking, especially with the assurance of support and training. "I'm willing to give it a shot," he said with a determined smile.

"That's the spirit, John! We're here to support you in your journey," Process Peters responded, pleased with John's decision. "Once you officially transition into the role, we'll tailor a learning plan to ensure you get the training you need."

HR Helen added, "And remember, this is a dynamic environment. Your role will evolve, and you'll have chances to explore various aspects of process analysis and related areas. Embrace the learning opportunities, and you'll continue to excel." With that, the meeting concluded, and John left with a sense of anticipation for the new challenges ahead.

The Dump

With the dust of the HR Helen and Process Peters meeting settling in the recesses of his memory, John's attention was now laser-focused on his new assignment. The exhilaration of his recent promotion and the accompanying responsibilities invigorated him. Armed with a comprehensive background briefing, he delved into the intricacies of the operations team, eager to make a significant impact.

In the heart of the operations department, five major areas diligently managed a range of pivotal organizational functions. Each area was a crucial cog in the well-oiled machine of the company, ensuring smooth and efficient operations across various domains and associated activities.

All these activities were meticulously organized and tracked through their in-house SAP-based application, PANDA. PANDA was a robust and versatile system, specifically designed to handle the complex needs of the operations department. It provided real-time data and analytics, enabling the team to monitor performance, track progress, and identify areas for improvement.

John marveled at the scale of operations managed by PANDA. The broader department juggled an impressive load, dealing with over 100,000 tickets per month, a testament to the efficiency and dedication of the operations team. This enormous volume of work was upheld by a formidable team of 1,200 employees and contractors, each contributing their expertise and effort to keep the wheels turning smoothly.

However, amid this well-orchestrated performance, there existed a mysterious quintet known fondly as "The Dump." This team, though small, held a unique responsibility. Tasked with addressing tickets that slipped through automation and evaded ownership from the major operational areas, The Dump was akin to a diligent caretaker. Their duty was to assess ticket contents and determine the appropriate course of action and team ownership.

John's current assignment and predicament revolved around a team that shouldn't technically exist—The Dump. Despite being composed of some of the most efficient operators in the operational domain, the team's creation was merely a stopgap measure to manage abandoned tickets. Over time, it had evolved into an operational overhead, lacking clear ownership.

The problem statement lay bare—the challenge was to identify the root cause behind the proliferation of abandoned tickets and devise strategies to render The Dump obsolete. This was the conundrum that awaited

John, beckoning him to unravel the mysteries and streamline the operational landscape.

Navigating the complex landscape of The Dump, John initiated his assignment by employing a classic technique from his academic arsenal—the Interviews and Surveys method. In this instance, John opted to forgo surveys and dove straight into the realm of interviews with the members of The Dump. Little did he know that this straightforward process would unearth a trove of insights that would prove both overwhelming and challenging to manage.

The members of The Dump, although well-versed in various facets of the overarching processes within the Operational Division, were deeply immersed in the day-to-day firefighting of tickets. Their focus was laser-sharp on comprehending ticket nuances and executing the necessary actions to ensure timely resolution or closure. This operational firefighting left them with neither the time nor the inclination to delve into the root causes of the deluge of tickets.

With an average monthly influx of 1500 tickets, the team found itself in a constant struggle to cope with the overwhelming volume. Taking time out to engage with John in discussions about potential gaps and root causes became a luxury The Dump couldn't afford. The urgency of their daily operational challenges overshadowed any contemplation of addressing the underlying issues contributing to the relentless tide of tickets.

Faced with the frustration of a seemingly uncooperative environment within The Dump, John made the decision to seek advice and guidance from his mentor, Process Peters. John received some valuable nuggets of process related advice from Process Peters but the most important of all was the list of techniques he could use or consider to solve his current predicament.

John learned that process analysis involves examining, understanding, and improving business processes. Various techniques are employed to achieve these goals and some commonly used techniques in process analysis can be found in the table below:

Technique Type	Description	Purpose
Flowcharting or Process Mapping	This technique uses graphical representations (flowcharts) to illustrate the steps, decisions, and interactions within a process.	Visualizing the entire process helps identify bottlenecks, inefficiencies, and areas for improvement.

Technique Type	Description	Purpose
Value Stream Mapping	Similar to flowcharting, but with a focus on mapping the entire value stream, including both value-adding and non-value-adding activities.	Helps to eliminate waste and streamline processes for maximum efficiency.
Swimlane Diagrams	Visual representation of a process that includes different lanes, each representing a participant or department in the process.	Clarifies responsibilities and handoffs between different parts of the organization.

Technique Type	Description	Purpose
Root Cause Analysis	A systematic process of identifying the underlying causes of problems or issues within a process.	Enables the elimination of the root causes to prevent recurring issues.
Process Metrics and Key Performance Indicators (KPIs)	Establishing and tracking metrics that measure the performance of a process.	Provides quantitative data to assess the efficiency and effectiveness of a process.
Interviews and Surveys	Gathering information from individuals involved in or affected by the process through interviews or surveys.	Gains insights into subjective experiences and perceptions, helping to identify pain points.

Technique Type	Description	Purpose
Benchmarking	Comparing your processes and performance metrics with those of industry leaders or competitors.	Identifies best practices and areas for improvement based on external standards.
Pareto Analysis	Identifying the most significant factors contributing to a problem by applying the Pareto Principle (80/20 rule).	Focuses improvement efforts on the most impactful issues.
Process Walkthroughs	Step-by-step review of a process with key stakeholders.	Encourages collaboration, uncovers hidden steps, and ensures a comprehensive understanding of the process.

Technique Type	Description	Purpose
Simulation Modeling	Creating a computer-based model to simulate the behavior of a process under different conditions.	Predicts how changes to the process may impact performance and helps in decision-making.

John learns that these techniques can be used individually or in combination to gain a holistic view of a business process and identify areas for enhancement. Given the current situation and task at hand, John could think of a few of these techniques that could be applied. Techniques such as Process Mapping, Process Walkthroughs, Swimlane Diagrams etc. seemed like obvious choices for John, however he faced the same challenge as before for all of them. The Dump team members did not have any existing documentation that John could use to start his analysis, neither did they have the time to show him how the processes worked. So, there was only one thing he could think of at that point that could give him a kick start - become a temporary working member of The Dump.

Hands-On Learning

Eager to delve deeper into the operations of The Dump, John approached Process Peters with his plan. "Process Peters, I'm finding it challenging to get the necessary insights from The Dump team. They're swamped with tickets and barely have time to talk about root causes. I'm thinking of joining them temporarily to observe and document the processes firsthand. What are your thoughts on this approach?"

Process Peters nodded thoughtfully, "It's an unconventional but practical idea, John. Immersing yourself in the daily operations will give you a unique perspective. You'll experience the challenges firsthand and gain a more intimate understanding of the processes. Just ensure you strike a balance between observing and actively participating. This hands-on approach might provide the breakthrough we need."

Feeling encouraged, John approached the team lead of The Dump, Manager Mike, to discuss his proposal. After explaining his intentions and emphasizing the short-term nature of his involvement, Manager Mike agreed to let John shadow the team. With that, John found himself transitioning from the role of a curious analyst to an active participant in the day-to-day workings of The Dump.

As he started this new phase of his assignment, John armed himself with a notebook, ready to absorb every detail and intricacy of the processes. Little did he know that this hands-on experience would prove to be a turning point in his journey towards understanding and optimizing the operations of The Dump.

It came as a great relief to John when he learnt that The Dump had some onboarding documents that were used to kickstart the learning journey of any new starters. These documents gave him the details he needed to gain access to the IT Systems the team were using to perform their day to day tasks. He also used the instructions to gain access to the various ticketing queues he could use to get a deeper and more meaningful insight into the type of tickets The Dump had to manage.

He spent his time, navigating through the tickets and getting his head around the processes he may need to touch or explore in order to action those tickets. Thankfully The Dump team members were very friendly and did not mind him asking questions as they worked through the tickets. For them it was the usual day work with commentary. They were closing tickets as per normal and educating John at the same time. A win-win situation for everyone involved.

Immersing himself in the world of The Dump, John soon discovered the intricate dance of handling tickets, addressing customer concerns, and navigating the complexities of the operational processes. As he shadowed team members, John started to identify patterns and bottlenecks within their workflow.

One day, while sitting with Ticketing Tam, a seasoned member of The Dump, John asked, "Ticketing Tam, have you ever thought about why we get so many abandoned tickets in the first place? Is there a common thread among them?"

Ticketing Tam glanced at John and replied, "Well, we're so focused on resolving each ticket quickly that we hardly get the time to look into the root causes. But I've noticed that a significant number of these tickets are related to recurring issues. It's like we're treating the symptoms, not the disease."

This insight sparked a realization in John's mind. He decided to delve deeper into the patterns of abandoned tickets, aiming to uncover the root causes rather than merely addressing the surface-level issues. As he continued his observation and hands-on experience, John felt a growing sense of confidence that he was on the right track to fulfill the expectations of his process analysis assignment.

As the days passed John had learnt a lot about the types of tickets that were coming through the queues of The Dump. He had become well versed with different scenarios that led a ticket to land in these queues. With the knowledge he has acquired over that past several weeks, he was feeling more enlightened and in control.

He started exploring other avenues, such as the resolution taken by the team for certain types of tickets. He started asking questions more around "what could have been done differently by the ticket creator so the ticket did not end up in The Dump". Since John had a lot more knowledge and understanding of the team and its processes, he was able to frame better and targeted questions. It was almost like he was very close to solving the mystery and John could sense it himself. Patterns had started to emerge and the information he had gathered thus far seemed to be paving the path ahead.

John's efforts began to bear fruit as he pieced together the puzzle of abandoned tickets. He conducted additional interviews with team members and, armed with his newfound knowledge, initiated discussions about potential process improvements.

One afternoon, during a team meeting in The Dump, John presented his preliminary findings. He mapped out the commonalities among the recurring issues, showcasing the patterns he had identified in the types of tickets that often landed in their queues. The team members were intrigued, and their curiosity grew as John delved into the analysis.

With each shared insight, John received valuable feedback from the team. They appreciated his fresh perspective and were eager to collaborate on finding solutions. Together, they brainstormed ways to proactively prevent certain types of tickets from entering The Dump, exploring preventive measures rather than reactive ones.

As the meeting concluded, John felt a sense of accomplishment. He had successfully integrated into the team, gained their trust, and initiated a collaborative effort to address the root causes of the persistent challenges they faced. The journey from being an observer to an active contributor in The Dump was a testament to John's adaptability and commitment to process improvement.

Over the coming weeks members of The Dump started to apply the "Push Back" strategy where, instead of acting on the tickets, they would determine why the ticket ended up in their queue and what could the ticket creator have done differently so the ticket went to the correct queue.

This was a cross team collaboration where members of one team were educating members of other teams. This strategy started to work as the volume of tickets coming over to The Dump started to reduce. When the monthly report for the ticket volumes came through Manager Mike was shocked to see that the ticket volumes had dropped by 30% in what was supposed to be one of their busiest months. He decided to monitor the ticket volumes on a weekly basis to determine if this was a once off. But to his amazement the drops in volume continued and by the end of the following month, the total volume had dropped by a massive 50%.

Manager Mike, seeing the significant improvement in ticket volumes, decided to hold a team meeting to acknowledge the achievements and discuss the positive impact of the changes. During the meeting, he commended the team's efforts, particularly highlighting the collaborative approach initiated by John.

As the team members shared their experiences with the "Push Back" strategy, there was a sense of pride and accomplishment in the room. The cross-team collaboration not only reduced the workload for The Dump but also improved the overall efficiency of the entire department.

In recognition of their outstanding efforts, Manager Mike decided to organize a team-building event to celebrate the successful implementation of the new strategy. The team members, including John, felt a strong sense of camaraderie and unity, realizing the positive outcomes that can emerge when different teams collaborate toward a common goal. The success of this initiative marked a turning point for The Dump and demonstrated the value of a proactive and preventive approach in their daily operations.

However, the members of The Dump were hit with a sudden realization – with ticket volumes decreasing, would there be enough work for them? Just as the team started to worry, Manager Mike shared some uplifting news that boosted their morale. Impressed by the success of John's project, the management decided to expand it to other parts of the business. This meant that The Dump team members could become Subject Matter Experts (SMEs) in their preferred areas and contribute to enhancing other teams within the larger operational unit.

Chapter 4

Transitioning Into Systems Analysis

Basking in the success of The Dump project, John found a newfound confidence that fueled his professional journey. Embracing an entirely novel challenge, he navigated it with an unconventional approach that proved effective, meeting the organization's expectations.

Now, John stood as the shining new star in the organization. Much to his immense surprise and amazement, he was honored with the Shining Star of the Year award by the management. This recognition not only acknowledged his outstanding achievements but also reflected the trust and admiration he had gained from his colleagues.

Process Peters, filled with pride, witnessed John's remarkable journey. Their professional relationship evolved, and Process Peters began to treat John not just as a rookie but as a trusted colleague. The success of

The Dump project had not only elevated John's standing in the organization but had also forged a lasting bond between him and his mentor.

Feeling the need for a new challenge, John continued to excel in every project assigned to him over the months. Despite his proficiency in processes, systems, and tools within the organization, the routine nature of process-related activities started to feel monotonous and less exciting for him. John harbored a desire to dive into technology projects, where he could contribute to designing and implementing new applications or enhancing existing ones.

While he possessed substantial knowledge about various applications and had become adept at process improvements, delving into IT implementation posed a new set of challenges. The intricacies of navigating this space as an analyst were less clear to him. Recognizing the need for guidance in this specific area, John set out on a quest to find a new mentor who could help him navigate the complexities of IT projects.

In one of their regular catch-ups, John broached the subject of venturing into the realm of Systems Analysis with Process Peters. While excited about the prospect of John exploring new horizons, Process Peters couldn't help but feel a twinge of sadness at the thought of potentially losing John to another department.

Having been entrenched in the same kind of work for nearly eight years, Process Peters understood the allure of comfort and the resistance to change. He, himself, had often entertained the idea of exploring different domains but found himself tethered to the familiarity of his role. Being the go-to Subject Matter Expert (SME) in the process area held him captive, a comfort that sometimes masked the desire for something new.

John, however, had a different perspective. He wasn't content with being a big fish in a small pond; he aspired to be a smaller fish navigating the vast ocean of opportunities. The prospect of exploring Systems Analysis offered him the chance to broaden his skills and embrace new challenges.

WORDS OF WISDOM

If given an opportunity, would you rather chose to be a bigger fish in a smaller pond and limit your options over comfort? or would you chose to be a smaller fish in a bigger ocean and explore the vast possibilities the ocean had to offer? the answer may depend on your personal circumstances but the choice you make will define your professional future.

– Anupamm Singh

Queen of the Technology Nerds

Systems Sarah, also known as the "Queen of the Technology Nerds," is an exceptional character who reigns over the Systems Delivery and Implementation division with unmatched expertise and charisma. Her presence is commanding yet approachable, a testament to her unique blend of technical prowess and personable leadership.

System Sarah's journey to royalty in the realm of IT began with her insatiable curiosity and passion for technology from a young age. She quickly moved up the ranks, her sharp intellect and strategic mindset setting her apart from her peers. With each promotion, she brought innovative ideas and implemented systems that revolutionized the company's technological capabilities.

As a leader, Systems Sarah is not just a manager but a visionary. Her leadership style is characterized by a perfect blend of innovation, precision, and a deep understanding of technological landscapes. She has a knack for identifying emerging trends and integrating them seamlessly into the company's infrastructure, ensuring that they stay ahead of the curve.

Under her guidance, the Systems Delivery and Implementation division has flourished. Systems Sarah fosters an environment that encourages creativity and continuous learning, making her team a powerhouse of tech enthusiasts. She understands that the world of technology is ever evolving, and she instills in her team the importance of staying curious and adaptable.

Known for her knack for turning complex technical challenges into opportunities, Systems Sarah is revered for her problem-solving skills. Her wisdom in navigating the ever-evolving tech domain has positioned her as a guiding force for her team. She believes in empowering her nerdy subjects, nurturing their talents, and challenging them to push boundaries. Her team, often referred to as the "Tech Knights," are fiercely loyal and motivated. They admire her not only for her technical brilliance but also for her empathy and understanding. Systems Sarah has cultivated a culture of mutual respect and collaboration, where every team member feels valued and empowered to contribute their best work.

Systems Sarah's influence reaches far beyond her division. She is a key advisor to the company's executive team, providing insights on how technology can drive business growth and innovation. Her strategic recommendations have led to the successful launch of several high-impact projects, positioning the company as a leader in the industry.

Outside of work, Systems Sarah is an advocate for women in technology. She actively participates in industry conferences and workshops, sharing her experiences and advocating for greater diversity in the tech field. Her efforts have inspired many young women to pursue careers in technology, contributing to a more inclusive and dynamic industry.

One sunny afternoon, Process Peters decided it was high time to introduce John to Systems Sarah. He believed that connecting John with Systems Sarah would be a valuable step in broadening John's horizons beyond the realm of processes, and provide him with insights into the technological innovations driving the company's success.

"John, I think it's time you meet someone who can give you a fresh perspective on our technological landscape," Process Peters said with a knowing smile. "Systems Sarah is one of our brightest minds, and I believe you'll benefit greatly from getting to know her."

Intrigued and excited, John followed Process Peters through the bustling office, eager to meet the legendary Systems Sarah. As they made their way to the vibrant, tech-filled kingdom where Systems Sarah held sway, the atmosphere began to change. The air was filled with the hum of servers and the soft clicks of keyboards, a symphony of digital activity that underscored the dynamic nature of the division.

They walked through sleek corridors adorned with futuristic artwork—abstract representations of circuits and binary code, interspersed with motivational quotes from famous technologists. The environment was a testament to the innovation and creativity that flourished under Systems Sarah's leadership.

As they approached Systems Sarah's command center, the aura of the place became even more pronounced. The command center was a spacious office with large windows offering a panoramic view of the digital landscape—rows of servers, workstations, and large interactive screens displaying real-time data and project statuses.

Systems Sarah's office, often referred to as the "Tech Throne Room," was both impressive and inviting. It was filled with the latest gadgets, cutting-edge hardware, and an extensive library of tech literature. Dual monitors on her desk displayed streams of code and project timelines, illustrating her hands-on approach and deep involvement in every project.

Process Peters knocked on the open door and called out, "Systems Sarah, I've brought someone for you to meet."

Systems Sarah looked up from her monitors with a warm, welcoming smile. "Process Peters, always a pleasure. And you must be John Smith," she said, extending her hand.

"Yes, it's an honor to meet you, Systems Sarah," John replied, shaking her hand and feeling an immediate sense of her charisma and energy.

"Please, call me Sarah," she insisted. "Come in, both of you. Let's sit and chat."

They settled into comfortable chairs around a sleek glass table. Sarah's office was filled with natural light, giving it a vibrant and open feel. The walls were adorned with accolades and framed articles about the projects she had led, showcasing her significant contributions to the company.

"John, I've heard great things about your work, especially your recent success with the stakeholder analysis, and The Dump" Systems Sarah began. "Process Peters speaks highly of you."

"Thank you, Sarah. I've been very fortunate to have such great mentorship," John replied, glancing at Process Peters, who nodded appreciatively.

Systems Sarah leaned forward, her eyes sparkling with enthusiasm. "Technology is the backbone of everything we do here. Our Systems Delivery and

Implementation division is where we transform ideas into reality. It's a place of continuous learning and innovation."

John listened intently as Systems Sarah shared stories of the division's recent achievements. She spoke of the successful implementation of a state-of-the-art cloud infrastructure, which had significantly enhanced operational efficiency and agility. She described how her team had tackled complex challenges, using advanced technologies and creative problem-solving techniques.

"What fascinates me the most," Sarah continued, "is how technology can drive business transformation. We are not just building systems; we are enabling new business models, improving customer experiences, and creating value in ways that were previously unimaginable."

Process Peters added, "John, Systems Sarah's team is a prime example of how we can leverage technology to stay ahead of the competition. I thought you'd benefit from seeing how they operate and perhaps find some inspiration for your own projects."

John nodded, feeling inspired by Systems Sarah's vision and leadership. "I'd love to learn more about your team's projects and see how I can apply some of these principles to my own work."

Systems Sarah smiled. "Absolutely. Why don't I give you a tour of our lab and introduce you to some of the team members? They're always eager to share their knowledge and passion."

They spent the next hour touring the division. Systems Sarah introduced John to her "Tech Knights," a group of highly skilled and motivated individuals working on various cutting-edge projects. John was particularly impressed by a team working on an AI-driven predictive maintenance system, which aimed to identify potential issues in the company's infrastructure before they escalated into problems.

Each team member they met shared their enthusiasm for their work and the impact it was having on the company. They discussed the tools and technologies they were using, from advanced data analytics platforms to machine learning algorithms. John asked questions, absorbing as much information as he could.

By the end of the tour, John felt a newfound appreciation for the technological innovations driving the company's success. He was grateful for the opportunity to see firsthand how Systems Sarah and her team operated and was eager to bring some of that innovative spirit back to his own work.

As they returned to Systems Sarah's office, she turned to John and said, "Remember, technology is a tool. It's the people and their ideas that drive progress. Keep pushing the boundaries, stay curious, and don't be afraid to take risks."

John nodded, feeling inspired and motivated. "Thank you, Sarah. This has been incredibly insightful. I'm excited to see how I can integrate some of these ideas into my projects."

Process Peters smiled, seeing the spark of enthusiasm in John's eyes. "I'm glad you two connected. I have no doubt that this experience will enrich your journey with us."

As they left Systems Sarah's office, John felt a renewed sense of purpose and excitement for the future. The introduction to Systems Sarah and her tech kingdom had broadened his horizons, giving him valuable insights and inspiration to carry forward in his career.

Systems Analyst

John and Systems Sarah met after a week in a sleek, tech-laden conference room. The room, with its state-of-the-art equipment and modern design, exuded an atmosphere of innovation and creativity. John sat across from Systems Sarah, eager to delve into the intricacies of the Systems Analyst role. The room buzzed with the energy of a dynamic team, the hum of servers and the soft glow of LED screens creating a perfect backdrop for their conversation.

Systems Sarah wasted no time in painting a vivid picture of what it meant to be a Systems Analyst. She leaned forward, her enthusiasm palpable. "John," she began, "a Systems Analyst is like the architect of our digital realm. We bridge the gap between business needs and technological solutions. It's a role that requires a unique blend of technical prowess and a deep understanding of organizational processes."

She paused for a moment, letting her words sink in, before continuing with an engaging tone. "Your primary task would be to analyze existing systems, identify areas for improvement, and collaborate with both business stakeholders and the IT team to design and implement effective solutions. It's about creating harmony between technology and business objectives."

Systems Sarah's eyes sparkled with excitement as she elaborated. "You'll gather requirements, create detailed specifications, and act as the translator between the language of the business and the language of technology. It's a role that demands creativity, problem-solving skills, and the ability to adapt to the ever-evolving tech landscape."

She gestured to the futuristic surroundings, "Our kingdom here thrives on innovation, and as a Systems Analyst, you'd be at the forefront of driving technological advancements within the organization. From designing new software applications to optimizing existing ones, your impact would be profound."

As she spoke, Systems Sarah tapped into the advanced touch screen embedded in the conference table, displaying a complex workflow diagram. "Take this project, for example," she said, pointing to the screen. "We're redesigning our customer support system to integrate AI-driven analytics for better issue resolution and customer satisfaction. As a Systems Analyst, you'd work closely with our AI specialists to ensure the system meets our business needs while leveraging cutting-edge technology."

Systems Sarah leaned back, a thoughtful expression on her face. "But it's not just about the technical side. Communication is key. You'll be presenting your findings, collaborating with cross-functional teams, and ensuring that the implemented solutions align with the overarching business strategy."

She continued, "You'll need to conduct thorough testing and validation to ensure the solutions you design are robust and effective. This involves creating test cases, coordinating with quality assurance teams, and iterating on feedback to refine the systems. Your ability to see the big picture and understand how each component fits into the overall business strategy will be crucial."

John listened intently, taking in the breadth and depth of the role. He could see the passion in Systems Sarah's eyes and the excitement in her voice as she described the challenges and rewards of being a Systems Analyst.

Systems Sarah concluded her overview by locking eyes with John, her tone earnest and inspiring. "It's a challenging yet incredibly rewarding role. You'll witness the tangible impact of your work, shaping the digital landscape of our organization. Are you ready to embark on this journey, John?" she asked, her voice a mix of mentorship and excitement for the possibilities ahead.

John nodded and said "Yes I am ready". His tone mixed with excitement and nervousness. He felt like it was his first day at work and the nostalgia of his early days in the company coupled with his early interactions with Process Peters gave him the enthusiasm which had started to fade in the process role.

Systems Sarah smiled and said, "Great to hear that, John. Welcome to the world of Systems Analysis! It's a dynamic field, and you'll find yourself working at the crossroads of business and technology."

Systems Sarah shared stories of successful system implementations, each one more inspiring than the last. She described the sense of accomplishment when a well-designed solution improved overall business efficiency, turning complex challenges into seamless operations. Her eyes lit up as she recounted these successes, and John could feel her passion for her work radiating across the room.

"One of my favorite projects," Systems Sarah began, leaning back in her chair with a smile, "was the overhaul of our logistics tracking system. It was a massive undertaking, involving coordination with multiple departments and external partners. The old system was clunky and inefficient, causing delays and errors that cost the company both time and money."

John leaned forward, eager to hear more. Systems Sarah continued, "We started by gathering detailed requirements from everyone involved, from warehouse managers to delivery drivers. The key was understanding their pain points and what they needed from the system. Then, we worked closely with our developers to design a solution that not only addressed these issues but also introduced new features that improved accuracy and efficiency."

She paused, reminiscing about the collaborative effort. "It was a true team effort. We had developers working tirelessly to build the system, project managers coordinating the timeline and resources, and end-users testing and providing feedback at every stage. There were late nights and intense brainstorming sessions, but the result was worth it."

Systems Sarah's expression softened as she added, "The best part was seeing the impact of our work. Once the new system went live, the improvements were immediate. We reduced errors by 30%, cut down processing time by half, and saved the company a significant amount of money. It was a proud moment for all of us."

John listened intently, absorbing every detail of the new world he was about to step into. The excitement began to replace his nervousness as he started visualizing himself contributing to innovative technological solutions. He imagined being part of a team that transformed business operations, solving complex problems with creative and efficient systems.

Systems Sarah then highlighted the collaborative nature of the work. "As a Systems Analyst, you'll interact with diverse teams, including developers, project managers, and end-users. Each group brings a unique perspective, and your role is to bridge these perspectives to create cohesive and effective solutions."

She pointed to another example on the screen. "In our recent CRM upgrade, we had to ensure that sales, marketing, and customer service teams were all aligned. Each department had different needs and priorities, and it was our job to balance these and find common ground. We facilitated workshops, gathered feedback, and iterated on the design until we had a system that worked for everyone."

Systems Sarah continued, "You'll be at the heart of these interactions, John. You'll need to communicate effectively, manage expectations, and ensure that the solutions we implement truly meet the needs of our users. It's about building relationships and fostering a collaborative environment where everyone's input is valued."

John nodded, feeling the weight of the responsibility but also the thrill of the opportunity. The prospect of working with such a diverse range of professionals excited him. He realized that this role would not only challenge his technical skills but also enhance his ability to work with people and manage complex projects.

"Communication is key," Systems Sarah emphasized. "You'll present your findings to senior management, conduct training sessions for end-users, and build strong relationships with stakeholders across the organization. Your ability to convey complex ideas in a clear and concise manner will be essential."

She smiled warmly at John. "It's a dynamic and rewarding role, John. You'll see the tangible impact of your work on the organization, driving efficiency and innovation. Are you ready to embrace this challenge?"

John felt a surge of confidence and determination. "Yes, Sarah. I'm ready to contribute and make a difference."

Systems Sarah nodded approvingly. "That's the spirit. Let's get you started."

Understanding the Role of a Systems Analyst

Definition: A Systems Analyst is a professional who plays a crucial role in bridging the gap between business needs and technological solutions within an organization. They analyze and improve existing information systems and design and implement new ones. Their work ensures that technology effectively supports the organization's goals and operations.

Key Responsibilities of a Systems Analyst

1. Gathering and Understanding User Requirements:

- **Requirement Elicitation:** Systems Analysts interact with users, stakeholders, and clients to gather detailed requirements for new systems or improvements to existing ones. This involves conducting interviews, surveys, and workshops.

  - *Example:* When redesigning the logistics tracking system, the Systems Analyst conducted workshops with warehouse managers, delivery drivers, and external partners to gather comprehensive requirements.

- **Documentation:** They document these requirements clearly and comprehensively, ensuring that all stakeholder needs are captured accurately.

o *Example:* After gathering requirements for the logistics tracking system, the Systems Analyst created a detailed document outlining features like real-time tracking, automated notifications, and integration with external partners' systems.

2. Creating Detailed Specifications:

- **Technical Specifications:** They translate business requirements into detailed technical specifications that developers can use to build the system. This includes creating data flow diagrams, system architecture designs, and user interface prototypes.

  o *Example:* For the logistics tracking system, the Systems Analyst created data flow diagrams showing how information would flow from warehouse entry to delivery confirmation, ensuring developers had a clear understanding of the system architecture.

- **Functional Specifications:** They also develop functional specifications, outlining how the system should behave, what functions it should perform, and how users will interact with it.

  o *Example:* The Systems Analyst wrote functional specifications detailing how users could input data, track shipments in real-time, and generate reports, providing clear guidelines for the development team.

3. Collaborating with Business Stakeholders and IT Teams:

- **Cross-functional Collaboration:** Systems Analysts work closely with both business stakeholders and IT teams. They act as a liaison, ensuring that the developed systems align with business objectives and user needs.

  o *Example:* During the CRM upgrade project, the Systems Analyst facilitated regular meetings between the sales, marketing, and customer service teams to ensure the system met all departmental needs.

- **Feedback Loop:** They facilitate a continuous feedback loop between the development team and the business users to ensure that the project stays on track and any issues are addressed promptly.

  o *Example:* The Systems Analyst organized bi-weekly review sessions where users tested new features of the logistics tracking system and provided feedback, which was then used to make necessary adjustments.

The Intersection of Business and Technology

1. Evaluating Efficiency and Effectiveness:

- **Current Systems Analysis:** Systems Analysts assess the performance of current information systems to identify inefficiencies and areas for improvement. This involves analyzing system usage data, performance metrics, and user feedback.

  - *Example:* The Systems Analyst evaluated the current customer support system, identifying frequent issues like slow response times and high error rates, which were impacting customer satisfaction.

- **Benchmarking:** They compare current systems against industry standards and best practices to propose enhancements.

  - *Example:* The Systems Analyst benchmarked the customer support system against industry best practices and found that integrating AI-driven chatbots could significantly improve response times and accuracy.

2. Proposing Innovative Solutions:

- **Solution Design:** Based on their analysis, Systems Analysts propose innovative solutions that improve system performance, enhance user experience, and align with business goals. This can include the adoption of new technologies, software updates, or process reengineering.

o *Example:* The Systems Analyst proposed implementing an AI-driven chatbot to handle initial customer inquiries, reducing the workload on human agents and improving response times.

- **Feasibility Studies:** They conduct feasibility studies to evaluate the practicality and potential impact of proposed solutions, considering factors like cost, time, and resources.

o *Example:* The Systems Analyst conducts a feasibility study to assess the costs and benefits of implementing the AI-based tool, including the expected return on investment (ROI) and implementation timeline.

Project Management and Strategic Alignment

1. Project Management Activities:

- **Planning and Execution:** Systems Analysts often participate in project management activities, such as planning, scheduling, and resource allocation. They ensure that projects are completed on time and within budget.

o *Example:* For the logistics tracking system upgrade, the Systems Analyst created a detailed project plan with milestones, deadlines, and resource allocation to ensure timely and efficient execution.

- **Risk Management:** They identify potential risks and develop mitigation strategies to address them, ensuring smooth project execution.

  o *Example:* The Systems Analyst identified potential risks like data security breaches and system downtime during the logistics system upgrade and developed mitigation plans, including data encryption and backup protocols.

2. Aligning with Business Strategy:

- **Strategic Alignment:** They ensure that the implementation of new systems aligns with the organization's overall business strategy. This means understanding the company's long-term goals and ensuring that technology investments support these objectives.

  o *Example:* The Systems Analyst ensured that the CRM system upgrade aligned with the company's goal of enhancing customer relationships and improving sales processes.

- **Performance Monitoring:** After implementation, Systems Analysts monitor system performance and user satisfaction to ensure that the system meets its intended goals and provides value to the organization.

o *Example:* Post-implementation of the logistics tracking system, the Systems Analyst set up performance metrics and surveys to monitor its impact on operational efficiency and user satisfaction.

Types of Projects Systems Analysts Work On

1. Developing Software Applications:

- **Custom Solutions:** They may work on developing custom software applications tailored to meet specific business needs.

  o *Example:* The Systems Analyst oversaw the development of a custom product lifecycle management (PLM) tool for the company's engineering team. This tool was designed to streamline the development process of new hardware products, integrating with CAD software and providing real-time updates on design changes, component sourcing, and production timelines.

- **Commercial Software:** They also evaluate and implement commercial software solutions, customizing them as necessary to fit organizational requirements.

o *Example:* The Systems Analyst evaluated and customized a commercial enterprise resource planning (ERP) system to better integrate with the company's existing customer relationship management (CRM) and supply chain management (SCM) systems. This customization ensured seamless data flow between product development, manufacturing, and sales departments.

2. Optimizing Existing Systems:

- **System Upgrades:** They propose and oversee system upgrades to enhance performance and add new functionalities.

  o *Example:* The Systems Analyst recommended and managed the upgrade of the company's existing customer support system to include AI-driven chatbots and machine learning algorithms for predictive customer service. This upgrade allowed the company to handle higher volumes of support tickets more efficiently and proactively address common customer issues before they escalated.

- **Process Improvement:** They analyze and optimize business processes supported by existing systems, ensuring they operate efficiently and effectively.

- o *Example:* The Systems Analyst evaluated the company's product return and refurbishment process. She identified bottlenecks in the reverse logistics chain and implemented a process improvement initiative that utilized advanced analytics and automated workflows to reduce processing time and improve inventory management for refurbished products.

3. Integrating New Technologies:

- **Technology Integration:** They explore and integrate new technologies, such as cloud computing, artificial intelligence, and big data analytics, to enhance organizational processes.

  - o *Example:* The Systems Analyst led the integration of a cloud-based Internet of Things (IoT) platform to connect and manage the company's smart home products. This platform allowed for remote monitoring, updates, and troubleshooting of devices, providing better service to customers and enabling the company to gather valuable usage data for product improvements.

- **Innovation Initiatives:** They lead initiatives aimed at leveraging emerging technologies to drive innovation and competitive advantage.

o *Example:* The Systems Analyst spearheaded an initiative to implement augmented reality (AR) in the company's technical support division. This project involved developing an AR application that allowed support technicians to guide customers through complex troubleshooting steps in real-time, enhancing the customer support experience and reducing the need for returns or technician dispatches.

Conclusion

The role of a Systems Analyst is dynamic and multifaceted, requiring a blend of technical expertise, problem-solving skills, and effective communication. By understanding and translating business needs into technological solutions, Systems Analysts play a vital role in driving organizational success and innovation.

Stop Dictating Solutions

John felt invigorated and eager to dive into his new role as a Systems Analyst. Systems Sarah's enthusiasm and confidence in his abilities had a profound impact on him. With renewed energy and a clear sense of purpose, John was ready to tackle the challenges that lay ahead.

Sarah took a hands-on approach to John's onboarding, ensuring he had a solid foundation to build upon. She provided John with access to a variety of resources and tools used by the Systems Analysis team. These included detailed documentation, project management software, and the latest analytical tools. Sarah also shared access to a repository of previous project reports and case studies, giving John valuable insights into successful implementations and lessons learned from past challenges.

To accelerate his learning, Sarah introduced John to key stakeholders involved in ongoing projects. These introductions were more than mere formalities; they were strategic connections designed to integrate John into the team and expose him to the real-world dynamics of system design, development, and implementation.

John's first few weeks were filled with meetings and discussions. Sarah ensured he had the opportunity to observe and participate in these sessions, providing him with a front-row seat to the intricate processes and collaborative efforts that defined their projects.

In one of his first meetings, John observed a brainstorming session for a new customer relationship management (CRM) system upgrade. The room was filled with a diverse group of stakeholders, including sales representatives, marketing managers, and IT specialists. Sarah led the discussion, skillfully guiding the conversation and ensuring that everyone's input was heard.

John took meticulous notes, absorbing the various perspectives and technical details. He noticed that while the sales team focused on features that would enhance customer interactions, the IT specialists were concerned with data security and system integration. Sarah adeptly balanced these priorities, highlighting the importance of designing a system that met both business needs and technical requirements.

Encouraged by Sarah, John began to contribute to the discussions. Leveraging his previous experience in process analysis, he identified potential areas for improvement in the current CRM workflows. He suggested streamlining the customer data entry process to reduce duplication and enhance data accuracy. His insights were well-received, and Sarah praised his analytical thinking.

As John became more comfortable, Sarah assigned him to a project involving the integration of an Internet of Things (IoT) platform for the company's smart home products. This project was particularly complex, involving both hardware and software components, and required close collaboration with the product development team.

Sarah arranged for John to shadow senior Systems Analysts working on the IoT project. He was given access to the project's technical documentation and design specifications, which detailed the architecture of the IoT platform and its integration points with existing systems. John spent hours studying these documents, familiarizing himself with the technical aspects and identifying key areas where he could contribute.

One of John's first tasks was to assist in the requirements gathering phase. He conducted interviews with product managers, engineers, and customer support representatives to understand their needs and challenges. John meticulously documented these requirements, ensuring that he captured every detail. He then collaborated with the development team to translate these business needs into technical specifications.

John quickly grasped the technical aspects of the IoT project. He identified several areas for improvement in the system workflows and functionality. For example, he noticed that the current design lacked a robust mechanism for firmware updates, which could lead to potential security vulnerabilities. John proposed a solution that included an automated update feature, ensuring that all smart home devices could receive timely and secure updates without user intervention.

Sarah was impressed with John's initiative and technical acumen. She encouraged him to present his findings and recommendations at the next project meeting. John prepared thoroughly, creating detailed diagrams and a clear, concise presentation that outlined the benefits of his proposed solution.

During the meeting, John confidently presented his recommendations. He explained the potential risks of not having an automated update feature and demonstrated how his solution would enhance security and user experience. The team appreciated his insights, and his proposal was quickly adopted into the project plan.

Sarah continued to mentor John, providing him with regular feedback and guidance. She encouraged him to take on more responsibilities and lead smaller sub-projects within the larger initiatives. John thrived under her mentorship, developing his skills and confidence as a Systems Analyst.

With each successful project milestone, John's reputation as a capable Systems Analyst began to solidify within the organization. His contributions were increasingly recognized, and colleagues began to see him as a reliable and innovative problem solver. This recognition was not just within his immediate team but across various departments, as his work often intersected with multiple facets of the business.

One particularly notable milestone was the successful deployment of the IoT platform for the company's smart home products. The project had been a significant undertaking, involving intricate coordination between hardware and software teams, rigorous testing phases, and careful planning to ensure a seamless rollout. John had played a pivotal role in its success, from gathering initial requirements to proposing and implementing critical system features.

As the project went live, the feedback was overwhelmingly positive. Users appreciated the enhanced functionality and security features, and internal teams praised the efficiency and foresight demonstrated in the project's execution. John's automated update feature, in particular, received commendation for its innovation and practicality.

John found himself enjoying the dynamic nature of the Systems Analyst role more with each passing day. He relished the opportunity to tackle complex problems, drawing on his technical knowledge and analytical skills to devise innovative solutions. The variety of projects he worked on kept him engaged and constantly learning. One day, he might be focusing on optimizing internal processes for the customer support team, and the next, he could be working on integrating new technologies into the company's product lineup.

The variety in his work meant that no two days were the same. John thrived in this environment, where each project brought new challenges and learning opportunities. He found satisfaction in seeing his solutions come to life, making tangible improvements to both internal operations and customer experiences.

As the days progressed, John grappled with the realization that the business's requests, while clear in their requirements, seemed to overlook crucial aspects of user experience and long-term sustainability. These requests, often driven by urgent business needs and tight deadlines, focused heavily on immediate solutions without considering the broader implications. John understood the importance of meeting these demands but was concerned that the short-term focus could lead to issues down the road, such as poor user adoption, system inefficiencies, and increased maintenance costs.

Despite his efforts to communicate his concerns tactfully, he found himself hitting a wall of resistance from stakeholders who were focused solely on short-term objectives. They were under pressure to deliver quick results and were often unwilling to invest the time and resources needed for more sustainable, user-friendly solutions.

John's first approach was to present data and case studies that highlighted the benefits of considering user experience and long-term planning. He prepared detailed reports showing how investments in these areas had led to higher user satisfaction, reduced maintenance costs, and better overall system performance in previous projects. However, his presentations were met with polite nods and appreciation for his thoroughness, but little change in the stakeholders' priorities.

Feeling frustrated but undeterred, John decided to take a step back and ponder potential strategies to bridge the gap between immediate business needs and broader strategic goals. He realized that addressing the underlying issues without alienating stakeholders would require finesse and diplomacy.

As a rule John started to ask two questions as part of his stakeholder engagements. At first these questions stirred the pot a little and stakeholders either were confused or got a little agitated with the line of questioning which they believed seemed unrelated.

Question 01: What business problem will this requirement solve for you?

Question 02: How will your proposed technical requirement align with the broader strategic goals of the organization?

During one of his early meetings using this new approach, John sat with the marketing team, who were requesting a new feature for their campaign management software. The feature would allow them to send bulk emails more efficiently. When John posed his first question, the room fell silent for a moment.

"Why does it matter what business problem it solves?" one stakeholder asked, visibly irritated. "We just need this feature to do our jobs faster."

John calmly explained, "Understanding the specific business problem helps us ensure that the solution we design actually meets your needs and provides value. If we know the exact issue, we can tailor the feature to solve it effectively."

Despite initial resistance, John pressed on with his second question. "And how will this feature align with the broader strategic goals of the organization?"

Another stakeholder responded, a bit defensively, "Our goal is to increase our outreach and engagement. Isn't that aligned enough?"

John nodded, "Increasing outreach and engagement is important, but we need to ensure that every technical implementation supports our long-term objectives, such as maintaining data security, enhancing user experience, and ensuring scalability. By aligning with these goals, we create solutions that not only meet your immediate needs but also contribute to our overall success."

Despite initial resistance, John persisted with his approach, convinced of its importance in bridging the gap between short-term needs and long-term strategic objectives. With each stakeholder interaction, he delicately posed his two questions, aiming to provoke deeper reflection and foster a broader understanding of the implications of their requests.

While some stakeholders initially balked at the unexpected line of questioning, John remained steadfast in his commitment to advocate for solutions that prioritized both immediate business needs and overarching organizational goals. He patiently explained the rationale behind his inquiries, emphasizing the value of aligning technical requirements with strategic objectives to ensure sustainable growth and success.

Gradually, John's persistence began to pay off. As stakeholders became accustomed to his probing approach, they started to appreciate the opportunity to consider their requests from a more holistic perspective. They began to recognize the importance of not just solving immediate problems but also laying the groundwork for future success.

One particular scenario still puts a smile on John's face. It was a quintessential example of how his strategic questioning could transform a routine requirement into an opportunity for significant improvement. John had been invited to a meeting with the products team stakeholders to gather their requirements for a new feature they wanted to implement.

As John sat in the meeting, he listened attentively while the products team stakeholders outlined their latest requirement: adding a set of product variants to a dropdown list in their online store. They described how this feature would allow customers to select different versions of a product, such as color and size options, directly from the dropdown menu. John diligently scribbled down the details, noting the specific product variants they wanted to include.

However, as he reviewed his notes, he couldn't shake the feeling that there was something missing—something deeper to consider beyond the immediate task at hand. With a thoughtful smile, John decided to pose his two critical questions to the stakeholders, curious to see their reactions.

"Before we proceed, may I ask two questions?" John began, looking around the room. The stakeholders nodded, expecting routine queries.

"First, what business problem will this requirement solve for you?" he asked, maintaining a neutral tone.

The room fell into a momentary silence as the stakeholders pondered his unexpected inquiry. They exchanged glances, and finally, one of them spoke up, "Well, it will make it easier for customers to choose the product they want."

John nodded, acknowledging the response, but he could tell there was more to explore. He proceeded with his second question, "And how will your proposed technical requirement align with the broader strategic goals of the organization?"

This question seemed to throw the stakeholders off guard. They looked at each other, clearly puzzled by the relevance of John's questions to their straightforward request. After a few moments, another stakeholder spoke up, "I'm not sure how this aligns with our broader strategic goals. We just need to improve the customer experience on the product page."

Undeterred, John smiled and replied, "Just curious. I think understanding the broader context can sometimes reveal new opportunities."

The stakeholder who had spoken first paused, considering John's questions more deeply. After a moment of reflection, he admitted, "You know, I need some time to think about this. Maybe we should revisit this discussion later."

John nodded understandingly, encouraging the stakeholder to take his time. "Of course. Take all the time you need. Let's make sure we're addressing the right problems and adding value where it counts."

Days passed, and John continued with his other tasks. Then, one morning, he received an email from the stakeholder. Instead of addressing the initial request to add product variants to the dropdown list, the stakeholder proposed a different approach: conducting a workshop to review the system's current flow and explore opportunities to enhance the user experience.

Grinning at the unexpected turn of events, John eagerly organized the workshop as requested. He knew this was a chance to dive deeper into the user experience and find more comprehensive solutions.

The workshop brought together the products team, UX designers, and customer service representatives. John facilitated the session, starting with a review of the current system flow and encouraging participants to share their insights and pain points.

As the workshop progressed, it became clear that the simple request to add product variants was just the tip of the iceberg. The team identified several areas where the user experience could be significantly improved. For instance, they discovered that customers often faced difficulties navigating between different product pages, leading to frustration and abandoned carts. They also noted that the existing search functionality was inadequate, making it hard for customers to find specific products or variants.

Inspired by these revelations, the group brainstormed innovative solutions to address these challenges. They proposed redesigning the product page layout to include dynamic filters and an enhanced search bar, making it easier for customers to find what they were looking for. Additionally, they suggested integrating a recommendation engine that would suggest related products based on customer preferences and browsing history.

John guided the team in prioritizing these ideas and developing a roadmap for implementation. The stakeholders left the workshop with a clear vision and a renewed sense of purpose, excited about the potential improvements to the user experience.

Over the following weeks, John worked closely with the development team to implement the new features. The redesigned product pages and enhanced search functionality were launched to positive feedback from customers. Sales metrics showed a noticeable increase in customer engagement and conversion rates, validating the team's efforts.

Reflecting on the journey, John felt a deep sense of satisfaction. His simple yet powerful questions had sparked a chain reaction, leading to significant enhancements that went far beyond the initial request. It was a reminder that sometimes, asking the right questions can lead to entirely new and innovative solutions.

As time passed, John's two questions evolved into a cornerstone of stakeholder engagements, transforming routine discussions into thoughtful explorations of the organization's strategic direction. With each interaction, John sought to bridge the gap between technical solutions and overarching business goals, driving alignment and clarity among stakeholders.

His unwavering commitment to driving positive change propelled him forward, even in the face of challenges. Through perseverance and dedication, John navigated the complexities of stakeholder management with grace and skill, earning the respect and admiration of his peers and superiors alike.

His strategic insights and unwavering dedication to the organization's long-term success did not go unnoticed. John became known not only for his technical expertise but also for his ability to see the bigger picture and guide stakeholders towards solutions that served the organization's broader objectives.

In the end, John's journey exemplified the power of thoughtful engagement, perseverance, and a steadfast commitment to driving positive change within the organization.

If You Cannot Explain It in Lay-Man Terms

John's journey within the organization continued to unfold, marked by milestones of growth and achievement. His dedication and contributions did not go unnoticed, and he was rewarded with a well-deserved promotion to the role of Senior Systems Analyst.

In his new position, John's responsibilities expanded beyond simply gathering requirements. He now played a pivotal role in providing strategic guidance to senior stakeholders, leveraging his deep understanding of both technical solutions and organizational objectives to drive informed decision-making.

But John's impact extended beyond his immediate responsibilities. Recognizing the importance of mentorship and knowledge-sharing, he actively engaged in supporting and guiding junior members of the team. Drawing from his own experiences, John offered valuable insights and practical advice on navigating stakeholder relationships and managing complex requirements.

Through his continued commitment to excellence and his willingness to invest in the growth of others, John exemplified the qualities of a true leader within the organization, leaving a lasting impression on both his colleagues and the broader organization as a whole.

On a normal looking day John got off his chair and headed towards the kitchen to fill up his water bottle. As John he his way down the hallway, a familiar sight caught his attention: several of his team members engaged in a heated discussion inside a meeting room. Curiosity piqued, he approached the door and gave a gentle knock.

"Hey, is everything alright in there?" John asked, concern evident in his voice.

One of his colleagues looked up, their expression a mix of frustration and exhaustion. "Not really, John," they replied with a sigh. "We've been dealing with a persistent issue of errors and bugs ever since we deployed that new product."

John's brows furrowed in sympathy as he stepped into the room, ready to lend a listening ear and offer any assistance he could provide.

He turned to the Systems Analyst, his brow furrowed in concern. "Were the requirements for this deployment clear from the start?"

"Yes, John!" replied the analyst confidently, but the developer's smirk hinted at a different perspective. John, sensing the tension, turned to him and asked, "You seem to disagree?" The developer shifted uncomfortably, then spoke up, "We have paragraphs after paragraphs of product description that make sense from a business perspective but not from a technical implementation viewpoint."

"Care to elaborate?" said John with a calm yet authoritative voice. The developer continued, "well we are dealing with a product that has multiple variants and each variant has a sub variant with overlapping properties with other variants. This keeps creating a conflict in the business rules and something or the other keeps breaking. We need clearer instructions on how to build the product structure in our data tables."

"Thank you for sharing," John acknowledged the developer's explanation before turning to the analyst. "How well do you understand the product?" he inquired. The analyst paused before responding, "Well enough, I suppose. However, without product managers available to explain the interdependencies between different variants and their sub-variants, I'm uncertain about what more I can provide the development team to design the product more effectively."

"Now that's a problem worth solving, isn't it?" Said John with a warm smile on his face. For starters let's look into this broader statement - What considerations should we have whilst building a product in an IT system? "Can someone get me started on the first point?" said John, as he picked up a whiteboard marker and proceeded towards the wall-sized whiteboard on the other side of the meeting room table.

As John started writing on the whiteboard, he felt a surge of excitement. He was about to embark on a collaborative journey with his team to tackle a problem worth solving. With a warm smile on his face, he turned to his colleagues and posed the question: "What considerations should we have whilst building a product in an IT system?"

One of his team members raised their hand, eager to contribute. "I think one of the first considerations is to ensure that we have clear and well-defined requirements," they said. "Without a clear understanding of what the product needs to accomplish and how it should function, we risk building something that doesn't meet the needs of our users or the objectives of the organization."

John nodded in agreement as he began to write "Clear Requirements" at the top of the whiteboard. Underneath, he added bullet points to capture key ideas as they were discussed. "Having clear requirements is essential for guiding the development process and ensuring that everyone is aligned on what needs to be delivered," he remarked.

The team continued to brainstorm, with each member contributing their insights and perspectives.

John facilitated the discussion, encouraging everyone to share their thoughts and ideas. Together, they explored considerations such as user-centric design, scalability, flexibility, security, integration, performance, and compliance.

As they filled the whiteboard with ideas and suggestions, John couldn't help but feel a sense of pride in his team. They were collaborating effectively, leveraging their collective expertise to address a complex problem and find innovative solutions.

The meeting had stretched on for what felt like an eternity, yet nobody seemed to notice the passage of time. Engrossed in their discussion, the team lost track of the hours slipping away. It was only when John glanced at his watch that they realized how late it had become.

"Goodness gracious, look at the time!" John exclaimed, a weary smile tugging at his lips. "Time really does fly when you're having fun, doesn't it?" His words drew a collective nod of agreement from the team, signaling that it was time to call it a day.

Gathering their belongings, John made a suggestion. "Let's pick this up tomorrow with fresh minds, shall we? We've got to get this release across the line." He paused for effect before adding with a touch of theatrical flair, "Defect Free." His melodramatic delivery elicited laughter from the team as they filed out of the meeting room, ready to tackle the challenges of the next day with renewed energy and determination.

John arrived at the meeting room a few minutes early, armed with a handful of whiteboard markers he snagged from the stationery cupboard along the way. Determined to make the most of the upcoming discussion, he set about preparing the room for the meeting.

With practiced efficiency, John connected his laptop to the meeting room projector and pulled up a PowerPoint slide titled "Things to Consider When Building a Complex Product Within an IT Application." As the rest of the team trickled in, he greeted them with a warm smile, eager to dive into the day's agenda and drive progress towards their shared goals.

"Good morning, everyone! I hope you all had a restful night," John greeted the team as they settled into their seats. "Yesterday's conversation was a great step forward in our journey to understand the nuances of product simplification," he continued, addressing the room with a sense of enthusiasm.

"I've taken the liberty of putting together a few slides outlining the core takeaways from our session. These aren't set in stone, but let's use them as guiding principles as we tackle the challenge at hand," John explained, gesturing towards the projected slides.

He glanced around the room, meeting the nods of agreement from his team members. "Is everyone ready?" he asked, seeking confirmation before diving into the day's agenda. The team responded with a unanimous chorus of assent, signaling their readiness to proceed.

"When building a complex product group within an IT application", said John "there are several considerations to keep in mind to ensure a successful design process and implementation." He clicked his mouse button to reveal the next slide. "Here are some key considerations we talked about yesterday". The slide revealed a list of considerations and their generalized definitions.

Clear Understanding of Requirements: Begin by thoroughly understanding the requirements of the product group. This involves engaging with stakeholders to gather comprehensive insights into their needs, objectives, and expectations.

Modular Design: Break down the product group into smaller, manageable modules or components. This modular approach simplifies the design process, making it easier to focus on individual elements and ensure cohesive integration.

Scalability: Design the IT application to accommodate future growth and expansion of the product group. Consider scalability in terms of both data volume and user capacity, ensuring that the system can handle increasing demands over time.

Flexibility and Customization: Build flexibility into the design to accommodate varying requirements and preferences across different product variants or subgroups. Allow for customization options that enable users to tailor the application to their specific needs.

User-Centric Design: Prioritize the user experience by designing intuitive interfaces and workflows that enhance usability and efficiency. Incorporate user feedback throughout the design process to ensure that the application meets the needs and expectations of its intended users.

Robust Data Management: Implement robust data management practices to ensure the accuracy, integrity, and security of the data associated with the product group. This includes establishing clear data governance policies, implementing appropriate access controls, and maintaining data quality standards.

Integration Capabilities: Ensure seamless integration with other systems and applications within the organization's IT ecosystem. This may involve leveraging standard protocols and APIs to facilitate data exchange and interoperability.

Performance Optimization: Pay attention to performance optimization techniques to enhance the speed, responsiveness, and overall performance of the IT application. This may include optimizing code, minimizing latency, and implementing caching mechanisms.

Compliance and Regulatory Requirements: Adhere to relevant compliance standards and regulatory requirements governing the industry or market in which the product group operates. Ensure that the IT application complies with data privacy, security, and regulatory guidelines.

As John listened to the team's feedback, he realized the importance of clarifying the underlying business requirements. With a few strokes of the whiteboard marker, he encapsulated the essence of the challenge: "Modular Design."

"One of the challenges we've been facing is around design components overlapping and causing errors," John explained, his words punctuated by nods of agreement from the team. "Would you say that's a fair high-level assessment of the problem statement?" he asked, seeking validation from his colleagues.

The developers nodded in unison, one of them elaborating further. "The code often gets confused when we try to merge two product variants into a singular offering," he explained. "This leads to errors and support tickets from the operations team."

John furrowed his brow, puzzled by the notion of merging products. "Why would we allow users to merge products?" he inquired.

A Business Analyst chimed in, providing crucial context. "Actually, this project involves offering a new product to our customers, allowing them to consolidate their older products into a single, more flexible offering," she clarified. "The goal is to provide users with the ability to migrate their legacy products to a new platform with enhanced features."

John's eyes lit up with understanding as the missing piece of the puzzle fell into place. "Thank you for clarifying," he said gratefully. "Now we can move forward with a clearer understanding of the business requirements." With renewed focus, he began mapping out the next steps to address the challenge at hand.

John listened intently as the Business Analysts responded to his questions, but he couldn't shake off the feeling of discomfort that settled over the room. "How many legacy products are part of this offering?" he inquired.

"Five," came the response from one of the BAs.

"Okay, great," John nodded, then turned to the next question. "And how many new products are on offer?"

"Just one," another BA replied.

John's curiosity piqued further. "Do we have a list of features offered by the five legacy products and the new one?"

Silence filled the room, thick with unease. Sensing the tension, John pressed on. "Well? Do we have a list?"

Finally, a Senior BA spoke up, breaking the uncomfortable silence. "Actually, we were given the product catalogue for the new product," she explained. "But the old product is so outdated that all the previous product managers have left the company. We couldn't find any literature to help us understand the product structure. And unfortunately, we have no subject matter experts to turn to for advice."

John took in the information, understanding the magnitude of the challenge they faced. It was clear that they needed to find a solution to bridge the gap in their knowledge and move forward with the project.

John turned towards the development team and addressed them, "Can you walk me through the current solution you have built? Just at a high level for now; I don't need all the intricate details just yet." One of the senior developers rose from his chair, grabbed one of the spare whiteboard markers John had placed on the table, and began sketching a diagram on the whiteboard.

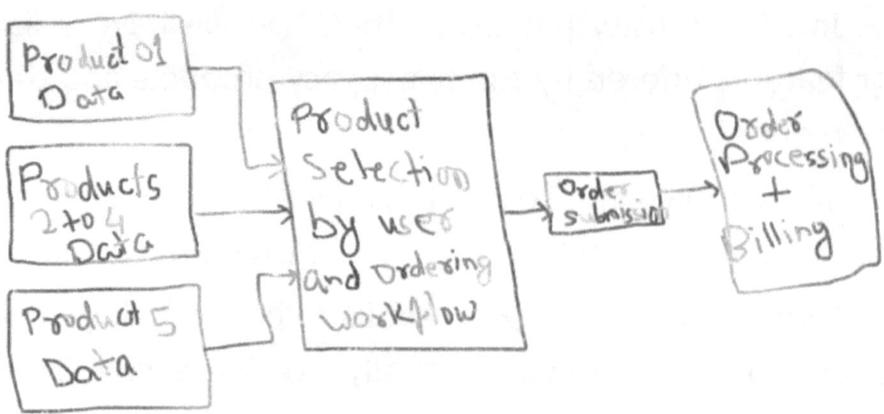

John looked at the diagram for a moment, absorbing its details, before diving into a series of questions directed at both the business analysts and the development team members. One question he posed made everyone sit up straight in their chairs: "Have we done a mapping of the fields available in the new product against the set of fields we have available in the legacy products?" One of the business analysts shot him a skeptical look, a mix of incredulity and uncertainty. Undeterred, John explained, "We want the new product to replace five legacy products, so it seems logical to compare their features."

The developers quickly voiced their agreement with John's suggestion, but the business analysts remained hesitant. "How can we compare five products against one?" questioned the senior BA cautiously, wary of dismissing John's idea outright. John acknowledged the challenge but emphasized the need to ensure the new product could accommodate the combined features of its predecessors.

Seeing the skepticism persist, John shifted tactics. Turning to the developers, he inquired, "Do we have a list of all the fields associated with each of the five legacy products?" One developer confirmed they did. "Would it be possible to obtain that list along with some sample data?" John asked. The developer assured him they could provide it by the end of the day in an Excel file. John smiled in appreciation.

As the meeting concluded, John felt a sense of anticipation tinged with excitement. He knew that what came next would set the course for a new chapter in his career. With the promise of data insights on the horizon, John's mind buzzed with possibilities.

Throughout the remainder of the day, John eagerly awaited the delivery of the Excel file containing the legacy product fields and sample data. When it finally arrived, he wasted no time in diving into the information. With each row and column he examined, John's understanding of the project deepened, and he began to see potential solutions taking shape in his mind.

Armed with this newfound clarity, John set to work. Late into the evening, he meticulously analyzed the data, identifying patterns and connections that would prove invaluable in guiding the development of the new product. As he worked, a sense of purpose and determination filled him, driving him forward with renewed vigor.

With each passing hour, John felt a growing sense of excitement for the possibilities that lay ahead. Little did he know, this seemingly routine task would mark the beginning of a transformative journey, one that would shape not only his career but also the future of the project and the organization as a whole.

Chapter 05

Simplicity is the Key to Success

The next day dawned with a new promise, and John was eager to gather with the team and tackle the complexities of their business problem head-on. He had spent the previous evening analyzing the data provided by the development team, and he couldn't wait to share his insights with his colleagues.

Deciding to add a touch of sweetness to the morning, John stopped by a bakery on his way to work and picked up a dozen hot jam donuts. With the tantalizing treats in hand, he entered the meeting room, where his team members were already engaged in lively conversation about their weekend plans.

Setting the tray of donuts on the table, John's gesture was met with smiles and exclamations of delight. As his colleagues eagerly helped themselves to the sugary delights, John sensed that the mood in the room was more relaxed and casual than usual. Wanting to capitalize on this light-hearted atmosphere, he decided to inject a bit of fun into the morning meeting.

With a mischievous twinkle in his eye, John approached the whiteboard and began to sketch out a table, listing a series of field names in each column. Turning to his team with a grin, he proposed a game of trivia. "Who's up for a challenge?" he asked, eager to engage his colleagues in a bit of friendly competition while they enjoyed their morning treat.

Let's Make It Simple and Keep It Simple

John scanned the room, his gaze meeting the eyes of each team member to ensure they were all on board. Satisfied with their eager nods and smiles, he launched into the game with enthusiasm.

"Alright everyone," John began, his voice carrying a hint of excitement, "I've taken some of the field names from our legacy products and given them new names based on the fields in our product order forms. Your challenge is to match each field with the correct product name. Write down your answers on a piece of paper."

With a flourish, John revealed the list of field names on the whiteboard, each one cleverly disguised with its new label. "You have ten minutes," he announced, his eyes sparkling with anticipation. "Once time's up, I'll reveal the correct answers along with the full field mapping excel sheet I've prepared."

As the team members set to work, scribbling furiously on their notepads, John couldn't help but feel a surge of excitement. This impromptu game was not only a fun diversion but also an opportunity to test their knowledge and problem-solving skills in a lighthearted setting. With a smile, he leaned back against the whiteboard, eagerly awaiting their responses.

John glanced at his watch and raised his voice to cut through the concentration in the room. "Two more minutes left, everyone," he announced, his tone both encouraging and authoritative. His eyes swept across the team, noting the varied expressions of focus and determination. Some had already finished, their pens paused expectantly over their papers, while others furrowed their brows in deep concentration, racing against the dwindling seconds.

With the deadline looming, a sense of urgency filled the room. Pens scratched hurriedly against paper as the final answers were hastily recorded. John watched with a sense of satisfaction, knowing that each member was fully engaged in the challenge.

"And... time's up, team!" John declared, his voice ringing out with finality. With a flourish, he lowered his arms, signaling the end of the task. The room fell silent, the tension palpable as everyone awaited the unveiling of the answers.

"Alright, how many people think they got all the answers right?" John inquired, his voice carrying a note of playful challenge. Two hands timidly rose in response, belonging to the senior developer and the senior BA. John's eyebrows shot up in mock surprise. "So, only two out of seven people got it right? Well, let's check the answers, shall we?" he said with a grin, gesturing towards the projected screen.

As the answers appeared on the screen, John observed the expressions of his team members with interest. Some nodded in satisfaction as their guesses were confirmed, while others furrowed their brows in contemplation. "Please take your time to assess your responses and ask any questions if there are any doubts or concerns," John encouraged, his tone warm and inviting.

By the time everyone finished comparing their answers, a subtle tension hung in the air. John could sense the shift and knew it was time to diffuse it. Clearing his throat, he addressed the room with a reassuring smile. "Well, there are no rewards for getting all the answers right," he began, his tone light-hearted, "but for those who did, well done. And for those who couldn't, I'm sure you've learned something valuable from this exercise."

Pausing for a moment, John continued, his voice steady and earnest. "The intent here wasn't just to test ourselves, but also to uncover any fundamental gaps in our design practices," he explained, meeting each team member's gaze with empathy. "Now, please don't get me wrong. I'm not suggesting that anyone did anything wrong here. Far from it. Instead, I want us all to consider how even simple changes in terminology within our data sets can confuse even the most knowledgeable of our end users."

As John spoke, the tension in the room began to ease, replaced by a sense of shared understanding and purpose. As the team listened intently, John continued, his words measured and thoughtful. "One of the fundamental principles in ensuring our users appreciate the benefits our technology systems offer is to make them understand that the system is designed to simplify their lives," he explained, his tone earnest.

"It's crucial to recognize that the average user doesn't grasp databases, datasets, or technical jargon in the same way most of us in this room do," John continued, meeting the eyes of each team member. "Our job is to bridge that gap, to translate complex technical concepts into language that's clear, intuitive, and meaningful to our users."

As John spoke, a sense of purpose settled over the room, the team nodding in agreement with his sentiments. "The good news is that we now have a real-life business problem that can serve as a platform to delve deeper into this concept and enrich our understanding in the process," John declared, his voice brimming with enthusiasm. "I must admit, I've never ventured this deeply into the realm of data before, and this project has not only captured my interest but also pushed the boundaries of my out-of-the-box thinking."

"So, let's dive right in and tackle this problem head-on by breaking it down into smaller, more manageable chunks," he continued, his eyes gleaming with determination.

Over the coming days, John and the team dove headfirst into the task at hand, rolling up their sleeves to tackle the intricate web of products, processes, systems, and data. Their goal was twofold: to simplify the tangled complexities and to navigate the delicate balance of the business world, which relied heavily on these foundational pillars.

With determination and focus, they meticulously dissected each component, meticulously analyzing its intricacies and interdependencies. Through collaborative brainstorming sessions and rigorous problem-solving, they began to unravel the knots that had previously confounded them.

As they worked tirelessly, their efforts began to bear fruit. Step by step, they untangled the complexities, smoothing out the rough edges and streamlining the processes. With each breakthrough, they gained a deeper understanding of the intricate ecosystem they were navigating.

Despite the challenges they faced, John and his team remained steadfast in their pursuit of simplicity and efficiency. Their dedication and perseverance were unwavering as they forged ahead, driven by a shared commitment to excellence and a desire to deliver tangible results.

And as they continued on their journey, they knew that every obstacle they overcame brought them one step closer to their ultimate goal: a streamlined, optimized system that would empower the business to thrive in the ever-evolving landscape of the modern world.

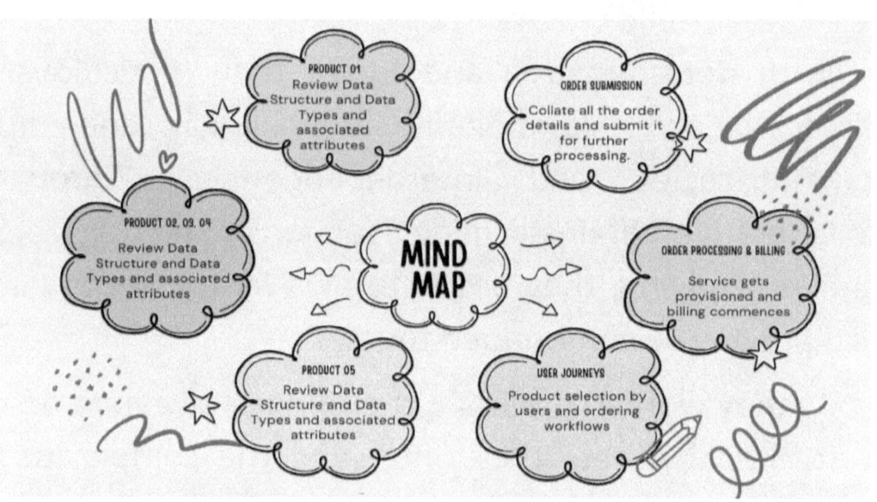

Case Study 01 – Case of the Complex Products

John and the team approached the business challenge with a refreshing perspective, opting not to adhere to a rigid, prescribed approach but instead relying on their intuition and common sense. Their methodology, while unconventional, proved to be highly effective, and their journey serves as a compelling case study for problem-solving in complex environments. The steps they followed are highlighted in this case study.

Step 01: Identify and Understand the Information Available

The initial step in the process involved identifying and comprehending the available information. The team recognized several key types of information that would be crucial for their analysis:

1. **Physical or digital product application forms for both the legacy and new products.** These forms provided insights into the specific details and requirements associated with each product, allowing the team to understand the differences and similarities between them.

2. **Process flow diagrams outlining the current business processes involved in managing the transition from legacy to new products.** These diagrams offered a visual representation of the workflow, enabling the team to identify potential bottlenecks or inefficiencies in the transition process.

3. **Table structures containing column names and field types used to store information related to each product type.** By examining the database schema, the team could gain a deeper understanding of how product-related data was organized and stored, facilitating the analysis of data relationships and dependencies.

By leveraging these types of information, the team could establish a solid foundation for their analysis and develop insights that would inform their approach to addressing the challenges associated with the product transition process.

Step 02: Convert Available Information in a Format that can be Easily Analysed

In the second step, the team focused on converting the available information into a format that was conducive to analysis. They followed these steps:

1. **Conversion of physical/digital application forms into Excel columns:** The team created a structured list of field names and corresponding field types for each application form using Microsoft Excel. This allowed them to systematically organize and document the information contained in the application forms, facilitating easier analysis and comparison.

2. **Compilation of fields and field types across the workflow:** Next, the team compiled a comprehensive list of fields and their respective types used at each step of the workflow. By breaking down the workflow into individual steps, they could identify the specific data requirements and interactions associated with each stage of the process.

3. **Mapping of field names against the database schema:** The team mapped the field names identified in the workflow against the field names present in the backend database. This mapping exercise enabled them to establish connections between the data elements used in the workflow and their corresponding representations in the database, facilitating data validation and integrity checks.

By completing these steps, the team created a structured framework for analyzing the data and identifying any discrepancies or inconsistencies between the different sources of information. This approach streamlined the analysis process and provided a solid foundation for further investigation and problem-solving efforts.

Step 03: Perform a thorough Gap Analysis

In the final step of the process, the team conducted a comprehensive gap analysis to identify discrepancies and areas for improvement. Here's how they approached the task:

1. **Comparison of legacy product fields:** The team meticulously compared the fields of the five legacy products, examining both similarities and differences to understand the scope of variation across the products.

2. **Creation of a combined field list:** They compiled a consolidated list of fields by merging the unique fields from each legacy product while eliminating duplicate entries. This consolidated list served as a reference for identifying common and unique data elements.

3. **Comparison with the new product:** The team compared the combined legacy field list with the field list of the new product to pinpoint any

disparities or missing elements between the two sets of data.

4. **Identification of gaps:** By analyzing the differences between the legacy and new product field lists, the team identified gaps in data coverage and functionality, highlighting areas that required further attention or modification.

5. **Scenario review:** They conducted a thorough review of potential process scenarios, considering the permutation and combination of merging two products at a time. This analysis helped anticipate challenges and identify optimal strategies for product integration.

6. **Blackspot analysis:** The team explored potential touchpoints within the processes that could lead to human errors or inefficiencies. By identifying these critical areas, they aimed to implement preventive measures to mitigate risks and enhance system reliability.

7. **Field mapping review:** They scrutinized the alignment between the field names used in the front-end interface and their corresponding representations in the backend database. This review ensured consistency and accuracy in data handling across the system.

Through these systematic actions, the team gained valuable insights into the existing gaps and challenges within the system, paving the way for targeted interventions and improvements to streamline operations and enhance overall efficiency.

Conclusion and End Result

The ten-week journey of thorough analysis and collaboration proved to be transformative for John and his team. As they delved deeper into the intricacies of the system, they not only uncovered a multitude of gaps but also forged stronger bonds among themselves. Communication flourished, fostering an environment of understanding and mutual support.

It all began with a sense of urgency and a determination to find the root causes of the system's inefficiencies. Daily stand-up meetings and cross-functional workshops became the norm. Each team member brought their unique expertise to the table, contributing to a comprehensive understanding of the system's intricacies. The atmosphere was one of intense focus and camaraderie, with everyone committed to the shared goal of improving the system.

Among the myriad of issues unearthed, one stood out prominently: the absence of a suitable solution to accommodate two critical legacy products within the new system. These products, responsible for a significant portion of support tickets, posed a substantial challenge due to their unique requirements. Their integration was crucial, yet the new system design had overlooked their specific needs. Additionally, the discovery of missing scenarios highlighted gaps in the system's design, leading to failures in subsequent workflow stages.

Despite the complexity of the issues identified, the team found solace in their newfound clarity. They realized that these problems, while daunting, were not insurmountable. Through collective effort and perseverance, they navigated through the maze of challenges, emerging with a clearer understanding of the system's intricacies and the path forward.

One particular brainstorming session stood out in John's memory. The team gathered around a whiteboard, sketching out the workflows of the legacy products. They identified key points where the system failed to accommodate these products, noting every detail. It was during this session that the idea of implementing flexible workflows emerged. These workflows would be designed to handle a larger number of scenarios, permutations, and combinations, ensuring that the unique needs of the legacy products were met.

The team embraced the idea and worked tirelessly to develop these flexible workflows. They divided tasks based on their expertise, with developers coding the new workflows, analysts testing them against various scenarios, and designers ensuring that the user interface remained intuitive. The process was intense, but the shared sense of purpose kept everyone motivated.

Additionally, John proposed incorporating a feedback loop from users earlier in the workflow journey. This feedback loop would allow the team to gather real-time insights and make adjustments before issues escalated. The team set up mechanisms for users to provide feedback at critical stages, ensuring that any problems were identified and addressed promptly.

As the flexible workflows took shape, the team tested them rigorously with the legacy products. They simulated various scenarios to ensure that the workflows could handle all possible cases. The testing phase was grueling, but it brought the team even closer together. They worked late into the nights, fueled by the shared goal of overcoming this challenge.

Finally, after ten weeks of relentless effort, the flexible workflows were ready for deployment. The team watched anxiously as they were integrated into the system. The initial results were promising, and as the workflows processed the first batch of data from the legacy products without errors, a wave of relief and pride swept over the team.

The culmination of their collaborative efforts yielded remarkable results: a staggering 90% reduction in support tickets. Despite encountering initial challenges and constraints, the team and the business alike recognized that the root cause lay not in flaws within the system or processes, but rather in design gaps within the new product. By addressing these gaps head-on and implementing necessary improvements, they had successfully mitigated issues that once plagued the system.

As they reflected on their journey, the team marveled at how seemingly daunting obstacles had transformed into manageable tasks. Their shared experience had not only improved the system but had also strengthened their bonds, setting the stage for continued collaboration and success.

The significant decrease in support tickets served as a testament to the team's dedication and perseverance. The newfound clarity and understanding paved the way for smoother operations and enhanced user experiences. Customers and internal users alike noticed the improvements, with feedback highlighting the system's increased reliability and user-friendliness.

With this achievement, the team embarked on a new chapter filled with confidence and optimism. Armed with valuable insights gained from their collaborative journey, they were poised to tackle future challenges with renewed vigor and unity. They had learned that by combining their skills and working together, they could overcome any obstacle and achieve remarkable results.

Chapter 06

John's Dilemma and Self Reflection

John sat at his desk, a furrow forming between his brows as he stared at the screen. It had been a challenging few months, filled with complex projects and tough decisions. As he reflected on his recent experiences, John couldn't shake off a lingering sense of unease.

He had always prided himself on his ability to navigate through difficult situations and find solutions to problems. However, lately, he had encountered a dilemma that seemed to have no easy answer.

The more he thought about it, the more John realized that his dilemma wasn't just about finding a solution to a particular problem. It was also about grappling with deeper questions about his role, his skills, and his goals.

Was he truly making a difference in his current position? Was he using his skills and expertise to their fullest potential? And most importantly, was he happy with the direction his career was taking?

As he pondered these questions, John couldn't help but feel a sense of frustration and uncertainty. He knew that he needed to find clarity and direction, but he wasn't sure where to start.

Taking a deep breath, John resolved to confront his dilemma head-on. He knew that it wouldn't be easy, but he also knew that he couldn't continue to ignore the nagging doubts and questions that had been plaguing him.

With renewed determination, John began to explore his options and consider his next steps. He knew that finding the right path forward would require courage, resilience, and a willingness to embrace change. But he was ready to face whatever challenges lay ahead, confident that he would emerge stronger and wiser from the experience.

Self Assessment Lite

John sat down with a pen and a notebook, ready to embark on his self-assessment journey. He started with the process discipline, reflecting on his experiences and achievements in this area over the past few years.

As he delved into his memories, John couldn't help but feel a sense of pride at how far he had come. From his early days as a rookie analyst, struggling to understand complex workflows and procedures, to his current role as a seasoned process expert, guiding teams through intricate projects with ease.

But despite his accomplishments, John couldn't shake off a nagging feeling of doubt. Was he truly living up to his full potential in the process discipline? Were there areas where he could improve, skills he could hone, knowledge he could deepen?

With these questions in mind, John made a list of his strengths and weaknesses in the process discipline. He noted down areas where he excelled, such as problem-solving and stakeholder management, as well as areas where he could use some improvement, such as time management and attention to detail.

Next, John moved on to the systems discipline. This was an area that had always fascinated him, with its intricate web of technologies and tools. Over the years, he had honed his skills in systems analysis and design, becoming proficient in understanding complex software architectures and integrating new technologies into existing systems.

But as he reflected on his journey in the systems discipline, John couldn't help but feel a twinge of uncertainty. Was he truly an expert in this field, or was there still much to learn? Were there new technologies emerging that he needed to familiarize himself with, or new methodologies that he needed to explore?

Once again, John made a list of his strengths and weaknesses in the systems discipline. He celebrated his successes, such as leading successful system implementations and driving innovation within his team, but also acknowledged areas where he could grow, such as keeping up-to-date with the latest industry trends and expanding his technical skills.

Finally, John turned his attention to the data discipline. This was an area that he had only recently begun to explore, but one that he found deeply intriguing. From data analysis to database management, John had quickly become enamored with the power of data to drive informed decision-making and transform businesses.

As he reflected on his experiences in the data discipline, John felt a sense of excitement and possibility. Here was a field where he could truly make a difference, leveraging his analytical skills and strategic thinking to unlock the potential of data-driven insights.

But as always, John approached his self-assessment with a critical eye. He noted areas where he excelled, such as data visualization and statistical analysis, but also areas where he needed to improve, such as data modeling and data governance.

By the end of his self-assessment, John felt a renewed sense of purpose and clarity. He had identified areas where he could continue to grow and evolve, and he was eager to embark on the next phase of his professional journey with confidence and determination. However, he also wanted to be thorough and precise so he could explicitly identify his own areas of improvement and interest. So, he decided to explore the various disciplines with a grain of salt.

John Assesses His Skills in Detail

John's approach to self-assessment was rooted in simplicity, aligning with his fundamental belief in the power of basics. With a clear focus on three core disciplines—Process, System, and Data—he embarked on a journey of introspection. Breaking down each category into its core components, he delved into the essence of his expertise. By meticulously evaluating his proficiency in these foundational elements, he sought to gain a comprehensive understanding of his skill set.

Beginning with Process, John examined its fundamental components, dissecting the intricacies of workflow design, optimization, and implementation. He then turned his attention to System, exploring the underlying architecture, functionalities, and integrations that underpin effective system design and development. Finally, he delved into Data, unraveling the complexities of data management, analysis, and interpretation.

But John's assessment didn't stop there. Recognizing the importance of practical application, he delved deeper into each category, identifying key tools and techniques essential for success. From process mapping and system modeling to data visualization and statistical analysis, he evaluated his proficiency across a spectrum of methodologies.

In embracing this methodical approach, John aimed not only to assess his current skill level but also to chart a path for continuous growth and improvement.

Core Components of a Process

The core components of a process typically include:

1. **Inputs:** These are the resources, materials, or information needed to initiate and carry out the process. Inputs can vary depending on the nature of the process and may include raw materials, data, or instructions.

2. **Activities or Tasks:** These are the specific actions or steps that need to be performed to transform the inputs into desired outputs. Each activity is usually defined by a set of instructions or procedures.

3. **Resources:** These are the people, equipment, tools, or facilities required to execute the activities of the process. Resources ensure that tasks are completed efficiently and effectively.

4. **Outputs:** These are the results or outcomes generated by the process after the activities have been completed. Outputs can take various forms, such as products, services, reports, or decisions.

5. **Controls:** These are mechanisms or checkpoints built into the process to ensure that activities are performed correctly and that desired outcomes are achieved. Controls may include quality checks, approvals, or reviews.

6. **Feedback Mechanisms:** These are channels or systems that provide information about the performance of the process. Feedback helps identify areas for improvement and ensures that the process remains aligned with its objectives.

7. **Documentation:** This includes any records, documents, or guidelines that capture the details of the process, such as procedures, specifications, or work instructions. Documentation ensures consistency and facilitates knowledge sharing.

By understanding and managing these core components, organizations can effectively design, implement, and optimize their processes to achieve desired outcomes and drive continuous improvement.

Common Tools and Techniques used by Process Analysts

Process analysts utilize a variety of tools and techniques to analyze, design, optimize, and manage business processes effectively. Some key tools and techniques used by process analysts include:

1. **Process Mapping:** Process analysts often use techniques like flowcharting, swimlane diagrams, and process modeling to visually represent and document current and future state processes. This helps in understanding the sequence of activities, dependencies, and decision points within a process.

2. **Root Cause Analysis (RCA):** RCA is employed to identify the underlying causes of process inefficiencies, errors, or bottlenecks. Techniques such as Fishbone Diagrams (Ishikawa), 5 Whys, and Pareto Analysis are commonly used to pinpoint root causes and prioritize improvement opportunities.

3. **Business Process Modeling Notation (BPMN):** BPMN is a standardized notation used for modeling business processes. Process analysts leverage BPMN diagrams to capture complex process flows, events, tasks, and decisions in a structured and standardized format.

4. **Process Simulation:** Simulation tools allow process analysts to simulate the behavior of a process under different scenarios or conditions. By running simulations, analysts can evaluate the impact of process changes, identify potential risks, and optimize resource allocation.

5. **Value Stream Mapping (VSM):** VSM is a lean management technique used to visualize and

analyze the end-to-end flow of materials and information within a process. Process analysts use value stream maps to identify non-value-added activities, streamline workflows, and reduce lead times.

6. **Process Performance Metrics:** Process analysts define and measure key performance indicators (KPIs) to assess the effectiveness, efficiency, and quality of business processes. Common process metrics include cycle time, throughput, error rates, and customer satisfaction scores.

7. **Process Improvement Methodologies:** Process analysts are well-versed in various improvement methodologies such as Lean Six Sigma, Kaizen, and Total Quality Management (TQM). These methodologies provide structured frameworks and tools for continuous process improvement and waste reduction.

8. **Stakeholder Analysis and Engagement:** Effective stakeholder analysis techniques are essential for understanding the needs, expectations, and perspectives of process stakeholders. Process analysts engage stakeholders through workshops, interviews, and surveys to gather insights and ensure alignment throughout the process improvement journey.

By leveraging these tools and techniques, process analysts can drive meaningful change, enhance operational efficiency, and deliver value to organizations across diverse industries.

Core Components of a Software Application

The core components of a software application typically include:

1. **User Interface (UI):** This is the part of the application that users interact with. It includes elements such as screens, menus, buttons, and forms that allow users to input data and receive output.

2. **Business Logic:** This component defines the rules and processes that govern how the application operates. It includes algorithms, calculations, and decision-making logic that determine how data is processed and what actions the application performs in response to user input.

3. **Data Storage:** This component is responsible for storing and managing the application's data. It includes databases, file systems, or other data storage mechanisms where information is stored and retrieved as needed by the application.

4. **Integration:** Many applications need to interact with other systems or services to perform their functions. Integration components facilitate communication

between the application and external systems, such as APIs, web services, or messaging systems.

5. **Security:** Security components are essential for protecting the application and its data from unauthorized access, misuse, or tampering. This includes features such as user authentication, data encryption, access control, and auditing.

6. **Performance Optimization:** Components focused on performance optimization aim to ensure that the application operates efficiently and responds quickly to user requests. This may involve techniques such as caching, load balancing, and code optimization.

7. **Error Handling and Logging:** These components are responsible for detecting and handling errors that occur during the execution of the application. They include mechanisms for logging errors, providing meaningful error messages to users, and gracefully recovering from failures.

8. **Configuration and Management:** Configuration and management components allow administrators to configure and manage various aspects of the application, such as settings, permissions, and user accounts. This may include administrative interfaces, configuration files, or command-line tools.

By incorporating these core components into their design, software developers can create robust, scalable, and maintainable applications that meet the needs of their users and stakeholders.

Common Tools and Techniques used by Systems Analysts

Systems analysts utilize various tools and techniques to analyze, design, and implement information systems that meet the needs of organizations and users. Some common tools and techniques used by systems analysts include:

1. **Requirements Gathering Techniques:** Systems analysts employ various methods to elicit, document, and prioritize system requirements, such as interviews, surveys, questionnaires, brainstorming sessions, focus groups, and observation techniques.

2. **Data Modeling Tools:** Data modeling tools like Entity-Relationship Diagrams (ERDs), Data Flow Diagrams (DFDs), and Unified Modeling Language (UML) diagrams help systems analysts visualize and document the structure and relationships of data within the system.

3. **Use Case Diagrams:** Use case diagrams are used to model and visualize the interactions between users (actors) and the system, depicting different

scenarios or use cases that represent the system's functionalities.

4. **Prototyping Tools:** Prototyping tools allow systems analysts to create interactive prototypes or mockups of the system's user interface, enabling stakeholders to provide feedback and validate requirements early in the development process.

5. **Business Process Modeling Tools:** Business process modeling tools help systems analysts map, analyze, and optimize business processes, such as Business Process Model and Notation (BPMN) tools, flowcharting software, and process simulation tools.

6. **Requirement Management Tools:** Requirement management tools help systems analysts manage and track system requirements throughout the software development lifecycle, ensuring traceability, version control, and requirement prioritization.

7. **System Design Tools:** Systems analysts use various design tools and techniques to create system architecture, including structured analysis and design (e.g., data dictionary, structured walkthroughs), object-oriented analysis and design (e.g., class diagrams, sequence diagrams), and architecture modeling tools.

8. **Unified Modeling Language (UML) Tools:** UML tools provide a standardized notation for modeling software systems, including use case diagrams, class diagrams, sequence diagrams, and activity diagrams, facilitating communication and collaboration among stakeholders.

9. **Requirements Management Platforms:** Requirements management platforms offer comprehensive features for capturing, analyzing, and managing system requirements, including traceability, impact analysis, and requirements prioritization.

10. **Collaboration and Communication Tools:** Collaboration and communication tools such as project management software, issue tracking systems, version control systems, and communication platforms (e.g., Slack, Microsoft Teams) help systems analysts coordinate with team members, stakeholders, and developers throughout the system development lifecycle.

These tools and techniques empower systems analysts to effectively analyze business needs, design robust solutions, and communicate requirements to stakeholders and development teams, ultimately ensuring the successful development and implementation of information systems.

Core Components of Data & Data Management

The core components of data refer to the fundamental elements that constitute data and its management within an organization. These components include:

1. **Data Sources:** Data originates from various internal and external sources, including business transactions, customer interactions, sensors, social media platforms, and third-party data providers. Identifying and understanding the sources of data is crucial for effective data management.

2. **Data Types:** Data can be classified into different types based on its format, structure, and characteristics. Common data types include text, numbers, dates, images, audio, video, and structured, semi-structured, and unstructured data. Understanding the types of data being collected is essential for data analysis and processing.

3. **Data Collection and Acquisition:** Data collection involves gathering data from diverse sources and formats, such as databases, files, APIs, web scraping, IoT devices, and manual entry. Data acquisition refers to the process of obtaining and ingesting data into the organization's systems for storage, processing, and analysis.

4. **Data Storage:** Data storage involves storing and organizing data in various storage systems, such as relational databases, data warehouses, data lakes, cloud storage, and distributed file systems. Proper data storage architecture ensures data accessibility, reliability, scalability, and security.

5. **Data Processing and Transformation:** Data processing encompasses the manipulation, transformation, and aggregation of raw data into meaningful insights and actionable information. This may involve data cleaning, filtering, integration, enrichment, normalization, and aggregation techniques to prepare data for analysis.

6. **Data Analysis and Analytics:** Data analysis involves examining and interpreting data to uncover patterns, trends, correlations, and insights that support decision-making and business objectives. Data analytics encompasses a range of techniques, including descriptive, diagnostic, predictive, and prescriptive analytics, to extract value from data.

7. **Data Governance and Management:** Data governance refers to the overall management framework, policies, and processes for ensuring the availability, integrity, security, and quality of data across the organization. Effective data governance involves defining data standards, roles

and responsibilities, data policies, and compliance measures.

8. **Data Security and Privacy:** Data security measures protect data from unauthorized access, disclosure, alteration, or destruction, ensuring confidentiality, integrity, and availability. Data privacy regulations govern the collection, use, and sharing of personal and sensitive data, requiring organizations to implement safeguards and compliance measures.

9. **Data Quality and Integrity:** Data quality refers to the accuracy, completeness, consistency, and reliability of data, ensuring that it is fit for its intended purpose. Data integrity ensures that data remains accurate, consistent, and reliable throughout its lifecycle, free from errors, duplication, or corruption.

10. **Data Lifecycle Management:** Data lifecycle management involves managing data from creation to disposal, encompassing stages such as data creation, storage, processing, analysis, archival, and deletion. Proper data lifecycle management ensures data remains relevant, secure, and compliant with regulatory requirements.

These core components of data provide a holistic framework for understanding and managing data effectively within organizations, enabling them to harness the power of data for strategic decision-making, innovation, and competitive advantage.

Common Tools and Techniques used by Data Analysts

Data analysts utilize a variety of tools and techniques to gather, process, analyze, and visualize data in order to derive actionable insights and support decision-making. Some common tools and techniques used by data analysts include:

1. Data Collection and Extraction Tools:

- **SQL (Structured Query Language):** For querying and retrieving data from relational databases.

- **NoSQL Databases (e.g., MongoDB, Cassandra):** For handling unstructured and semi-structured data.

- **Web Scraping Tools (e.g., BeautifulSoup, Scrapy):** For extracting data from websites and online sources.

- **APIs (Application Programming Interfaces):** For accessing and retrieving data from web services and applications.

2. Data Cleaning and Preparation Tools:

- **Excel:** For basic data cleaning, formatting, and manipulation tasks.

- **OpenRefine:** For cleaning and transforming messy data, handling missing values, and standardizing data formats.

- **Trifacta Wrangler:** For visually exploring and cleaning data through an intuitive interface.

- **Pandas:** Python library for data manipulation and analysis, including cleaning, filtering, and transforming data.

3. Data Analysis and Statistical Tools:

- **R:** Programming language and environment for statistical computing and data analysis.

- **Python:** Along with libraries such as NumPy, SciPy, and StatsModels for statistical analysis and modeling.

- **MATLAB:** For advanced numerical computing, data analysis, and visualization.

- **SPSS (Statistical Package for the Social Sciences):** For statistical analysis, data mining, and predictive modeling.

4. Data Visualization Tools:

- **Tableau:** For creating interactive and visually appealing data visualizations and dashboards.

- **Power BI (Microsoft Power BI):** Business analytics tool for data visualization, reporting, and sharing insights.

- **matplotlib and Seaborn:** Python libraries for creating static and interactive visualizations.

- **ggplot2:** R package for producing elegant and customizable plots and charts.

5. Machine Learning and Predictive Analytics Tools:

- **Scikit-learn:** Python library for machine learning algorithms, including classification, regression, clustering, and dimensionality reduction.

- **TensorFlow and Keras:** Deep learning frameworks for building and training neural networks.

- **Weka:** Data mining software with a collection of machine learning algorithms and tools for predictive modeling.

- **RapidMiner:** Integrated platform for data science, including machine learning, text mining, and predictive analytics.

6. Big Data and Distributed Computing Tools:

- **Hadoop:** Distributed storage and processing framework for handling large-scale datasets.

- **Spark:** Fast and general-purpose cluster computing system for big data processing and analytics.

- **Apache Hive and Apache Pig:** Tools for querying and analyzing large datasets stored in Hadoop.

- **Apache Kafka:** Distributed streaming platform for handling real-time data streams and event processing.

7. **Text Analytics and Natural Language Processing (NLP) Tools:**

- **NLTK (Natural Language Toolkit):** Python library for text analysis and NLP tasks such as tokenization, stemming, and sentiment analysis.

- **spaCy:** Python library for advanced NLP tasks including named entity recognition, part-of-speech tagging, and dependency parsing.

- **Gensim:** Library for topic modeling, document similarity analysis, and other text analytics tasks.

These tools and techniques provide data analysts with the necessary capabilities to explore, analyze, and derive insights from data across various domains and industries. Depending on the specific requirements of their projects, data analysts may employ a combination of these tools to effectively address data-related challenges and drive informed decision-making.

Where-To From Here?

John's realization was a sobering moment. Despite his years of experience and dedication to his craft, the assessment revealed gaps in his skills across the three disciplines of process analysis, systems analysis, and data analysis. It was a humbling experience, but John saw it as an opportunity for growth and self-improvement.

As he reviewed the graded scoring system and reflected on his performance, John understood that mastery in each discipline required continuous learning and adaptation. He acknowledged that the ever-evolving nature of technology and business demanded constant upskilling and refinement of skills.

Rather than feeling discouraged, John embraced the assessment results as a catalyst for personal and professional development. He made a commitment to invest time and effort into enhancing his expertise in areas where he fell short. Whether through self-study, online courses, or seeking mentorship from experienced professionals, John was determined to bridge the gap between his current skill level and the proficiency he aspired to achieve.

Moreover, John recognized the value of interdisciplinary knowledge and the importance of being well-rounded in today's dynamic work environment. By broadening his skill set across multiple disciplines, he aimed to become a versatile and adaptable asset to his organization.

In the end, John's assessment served as a wake-up call, prompting him to embark on a journey of continuous learning and growth. With perseverance and a proactive mindset, he was confident that he could overcome his shortcomings and emerge as a stronger, more capable professional in the years to come.

John's self-assessment was a pivotal moment that brought clarity to his understanding of professional growth. As he reflected on the results, he came to a profound realization: mastery of all disciplines was an unattainable feat, given the rapid pace of change in the business and technology landscape.

The dynamic nature of the industry meant that no matter how much he improved his skills, there would always be new developments, emerging technologies, and evolving methodologies to contend with. Rather than feeling disheartened by this reality, John embraced it as an inherent aspect of professional growth.

He understood that the key to success lay not in trying to master every discipline, but in cultivating a mindset of continuous adaptation and learning. By remaining agile and open to new ideas, John could navigate the ever-changing landscape with confidence and resilience.

Moreover, John recognized that focusing on his strengths and areas of passion would yield greater dividends than attempting to excel in every facet of his profession. By honing his expertise in select areas and staying abreast of industry trends, he could position himself as a valuable asset in the marketplace.

The self-assessment exercise served as a catalyst for John's personal and professional development journey. It instilled in him a sense of humility, curiosity, and determination to embrace change and pursue growth relentlessly.

John's quest for clarity led him to ponder a fundamental question: What truly inspired him to rise each morning? He yearned to identify his passions and chart a course toward a fulfilling career path.

To navigate this introspective journey, John knew he needed a structured approach. He began by reflecting on his past experiences, recalling moments of genuine enthusiasm and satisfaction. He explored the tasks and projects that ignited his curiosity and sparked a sense of purpose within him.

Next, John engaged in soul-searching conversations with trusted mentors, friends, and family members. He knew that his journey towards clarity and fulfillment couldn't be undertaken alone. The insights and perspectives of those who knew him best could offer valuable guidance and help him uncover hidden talents and interests he may have overlooked.

John's first conversation was with Systems Sarah, his mentor and role model. They met at their favorite coffee shop, a cozy corner spot with a view of the bustling city streets. As they sipped their drinks, John opened up about his recent struggles and doubts.

"Sarah, I've been feeling lost lately," he confessed. "I'm not sure if I'm making the impact I want, or if I'm even heading in the right direction."

Sarah listened intently, her eyes full of empathy. "John, it's natural to feel this way at times. Your dedication and passion are evident, but it's important to reassess and realign your goals periodically. Sometimes, we get so caught up in the day-to-day that we lose sight of the bigger picture."

She then shared stories from her own career, recounting moments of doubt and uncertainty she had faced. "There were times when I questioned my path, too," she admitted. "But those moments pushed me to explore new opportunities and discover hidden strengths. You have so much potential, John. It's about finding where you can make the most difference."

Encouraged by Systems Sarah's wisdom, John decided to seek more perspectives. He reached out to old friends from college, organizing a casual get-together at a local park. As they walked and talked, John shared his feelings of uncertainty and listened as his friends shared their own career journeys.

One friend, Algorithm Alex, a software developer, spoke about a time when he felt stuck in a monotonous job. "I realized I needed a change, so I started exploring new fields. I took some online courses in AI and machine learning, and now I'm working on projects that I'm truly passionate about. Sometimes, stepping out of your comfort zone can lead to amazing discoveries."

John was inspired by his friends' stories. He realized that he, too, needed to explore and be open to new opportunities. He began to see his current situation not as a dead end, but as a crossroads offering multiple paths.

Another pivotal conversation was with Process Peters, his colleague and another trusted mentor. They met in the office's break room, where they often had candid discussions over coffee. John shared his feelings of uncertainty and the internal struggle he had been facing.

"Process Peters, I feel like I'm not making the impact I want. I'm questioning my role and whether I'm truly using my skills to their fullest potential."

Process Peters nodded thoughtfully. "John, I've seen you handle some of the toughest challenges we've faced. Your problem-solving skills are exceptional, but sometimes, it's about finding the right context to apply them. Have you considered exploring different areas within the organization or even looking into advanced roles?"

He continued, "When I was at a similar crossroads, I took on projects outside my usual scope. It helped me discover new interests and skills. Maybe it's time to step out of your comfort zone and tackle something new."

John appreciated Process Peter's practical advice. He decided to take actionable steps based on the guidance he received from both Sarah and Peters. He enrolled in a course on data analytics, a field that had always intrigued him but that he had never fully explored. He also began attending industry meetups and networking events, looking for opportunities to connect with professionals in different fields.

Embracing a spirit of experimentation, John dabbled in various domains and disciplines, seeking opportunities to test his skills and gauge his level of engagement. Whether it was diving into new projects at work, volunteering for community initiatives, or pursuing personal hobbies, John embraced every experience as a chance to discover his true passions.

As he embarked on this journey of self-discovery, John remained open-minded and adaptable, knowing that clarity would emerge gradually, through a combination of exploration, reflection, and introspection. With each step forward, he grew closer to unraveling the mystery of his inner drive and finding his purpose in life.

Chapter 07

The Problem Solver

Almost a year had passed since John undertook his self-assessment journey. During this time, he actively sought feedback from his supervisors and colleagues to gauge his professional strengths and weaknesses. Consistently, the responses he received echoed a familiar theme - appreciation for his dedication, intellect, and collaborative spirit in project delivery. While this feedback affirmed his abilities and fueled his ongoing growth, John remained introspective, searching for a succinct way to encapsulate his professional identity. If he were to distill his essence into a couple of words, what would they be?

Lost in his own thoughts, John stood in line at the office cafeteria, oblivious to his surroundings. A tap on his shoulder jolted him back to reality, and he turned to see Process Peters, a familiar face from the office. Chuckling at John's absent-minded demeanor, Process Peters couldn't help but remark on his friend's distracted state. "Hey John, you look like you've seen a ghost! Everything alright?" John quickly shook off his reverie and offered an apologetic smile. "Sorry, Pete," he replied sheepishly, "I was lost in my own thoughts. Didn't mean to zone out like that." With a friendly nod, Process Peters placed his order, but his concerned expression lingered as he joined John at the counter.

As they waited for their meals, Process Peters couldn't help but notice the weight of concern that seemed to hang over John's shoulders. "Is everything okay, John?" he asked gently, his tone laced with genuine concern. John hesitated for a moment, unsure of how to articulate the thoughts that had been swirling in his mind. Finally, he sighed and met Process Peters gaze. "Honestly, Pete, I've been doing a lot of soul-searching lately," he admitted, his voice tinged with uncertainty. "I feel like I've reached a bit of a crossroads in my career, and I'm not sure which path to take." Process Peters listened attentively, his expression sympathetic. "It's natural to feel that way, John," he reassured him. "We all go through periods of uncertainty. But remember, it's okay to take a step back and reevaluate your goals."

John nodded, grateful for Process Peters understanding. "Thanks, Pete," he said sincerely.

"I guess I just need to figure out what truly drives me, you know? What makes me excited to come to work every day." Process Peters offered a reassuring smile. "You'll find your way, John," he said confidently. "Just give yourself the time and space to explore your options. And remember, I'm always here if you need someone to bounce ideas off of." With a sense of gratitude and renewed determination, John collected his lunch and made his way towards the dinning area alongside Process Peters.

As John and Process Peters settled at a nearby table, John's spirits lifted as they engaged in conversation about work and life. With each exchange, John found himself drawn out of his earlier contemplative state, buoyed by Process Peters' easy demeanor and genuine interest. They shared insights, anecdotes, and even a few laughs, the conversation flowing effortlessly between them.

However, their interaction was abruptly interrupted when Process Peters glanced at his phone, his expression shifting to one of sudden urgency. "Sorry, John," he exclaimed, rising from his seat, "I've got to run. Late for a meeting." Before John could respond, Process Peters turned back to him with a proposition. "Hey, are you free tomorrow? I could really use your input on a business problem I've been grappling with. Just an hour or so of your time would be incredibly helpful."

John nodded eagerly, a spark of excitement igniting within him at the prospect of contributing his insights. "Of course," he replied with a smile. "I'll keep my schedule clear. Just send over the details, and I'll be there." Process Peters grinned appreciatively. "Fantastic! I'll send out a meeting invite right away. Thanks, John. And remember, don't sweat the small stuff. See you tomorrow." With that, Process Peters hurried off, leaving John feeling invigorated and eager for the challenges that lay ahead.

John returned to his desk, his mind buzzing with anticipation. He settled into his chair and opened his work laptop, greeted by the familiar hum of its startup. As he logged into his email account, his eyes were immediately drawn to the bold subject line at the top of his inbox: "Meeting Invitation: Business Problem Discussion."

His heart skipped a beat as he clicked on the invitation from Process Peters. The meeting was scheduled for tomorrow morning, and although the agenda was brief, John felt a surge of excitement. He knew that any discussion with Process Peters was bound to be engaging and thought-provoking.

With a sense of purpose, John accepted the invitation and marked the meeting on his calendar. He couldn't help but wonder about the nature of the business problem they would be discussing and how he could contribute to finding a solution. As he closed his laptop, John felt a renewed sense of energy and determination. Tomorrow couldn't come soon enough.

Case Study #2 – The Case of Too Many Support Tickets

As John woke up and began his morning routine, a sense of anticipation filled him. Today was not just another day at the office; it held the promise of clarity and purpose. Over the past few years, John had found himself drifting, unsure of his path amidst the endless stream of projects. But today's meeting with Process Peters represented a chance for him to find his bearings and rediscover his true calling.

With a spring in his step, John made his way to work, his mind buzzing with possibilities. Along the way, he stopped by the food truck stationed across from his office building, indulging in his newfound ritual of picking up a bag of hot jam donuts. It was a small gesture, but one that brought him comfort and a sense of camaraderie before important meetings.

Arriving at his desk, John went through his usual routine of checking emails and calendar appointments. With a quick glance at his schedule, he confirmed the upcoming meeting with Process Peters and made his way to the designated meeting room on Level 10. As he walked, he couldn't help but feel a surge of excitement mingled with nervous anticipation. Today held the promise of clarity, and John was ready to seize it.

As John stepped into the meeting room, he was greeted by the sight of Process Peters and Systems Sarah already seated, their faces alight with warm smiles. With a friendly "good morning," they welcomed John, who reciprocated with equal warmth. Placing the bag of hot jam donuts on the table, John invited them to help themselves, prompting Systems Sarah to inquire about the occasion.

With a casual shrug, John explained, "Just a small token of appreciation for this opportunity and for your unwavering support throughout my journey." Both Process Peters and Systems Sarah nodded in gratitude, their appreciation evident. After a brief exchange of pleasantries and a shared indulgence in the sweet treats, John's curiosity got the better of him.

Leaning forward, he addressed his mentors with an inquisitive gaze. "So, what's the challenge we're facing? What's on the agenda today?"

The Problem

In the operational support department overseen by Systems Sarah, a noticeable uptick in ticket volume had been observed over the past few months. What was once a manageable flow of requests had gradually evolved into a steady stream, placing increased pressure on her team to keep up with the growing demand.

As the manager of the support team, Systems Sarah recognized the need to address this escalating trend before it became overwhelming. With the number of tickets rising steadily, she knew that proactive measures were necessary to maintain the efficiency and effectiveness of their support operations.

This surge in ticket volume had implications beyond just the workload of her team. It also raised concerns about potential bottlenecks in the organization's processes or systems that might be contributing to the increase in support requests. Systems Sarah understood the importance of identifying and addressing these underlying issues to prevent further strain on her team and ensure smooth operations across the board.

Moreover, she was mindful of the impact that prolonged periods of high workload could have on her team's morale and productivity. Addressing the root causes of the increased ticket volume was not only essential for maintaining operational efficiency but also for fostering a positive work environment and ensuring the well-being of her team members.

Brainstorming – Let's Identify the Root Cause

John's curiosity was piqued by the potential correlation between the surge in ticket volume and the recent system upgrades. He grasped a whiteboard marker, ready to unravel the mystery. "So the problem has grown over the past few months, but do we know when the numbers started to grow? There has to be an event or trigger that would have instigated this growth in ticket numbers."

Systems Sarah nodded in agreement, acknowledging John's keen observation. "Well, looking at the type of tickets we are receiving, I suspect this could have been triggered by one of the two system upgrades we made around six months ago. There is a chance that either one of those upgrades or possibly both might be contributing towards this issue."

John furrowed his brow in concentration as he began jotting down notes on the whiteboard. "What were those upgrades?" he inquired, eager to uncover any potential links between the system changes and the surge in support requests.

Systems Sarah began to outline the details. "The first upgrade was a major overhaul of our user interface, aiming to make the system more intuitive and user-friendly. The second upgrade involved the integration of a new backend system designed to improve data processing and overall performance."

John nodded thoughtfully, writing "User Interface Upgrade" and "Backend Integration" on the whiteboard. "Let's break this down further," he said. "What specific changes did the UI upgrade entail?"

Systems Sarah responded, "We redesigned the dashboard, added new navigation features, and simplified the input forms. While the feedback has been generally positive, there have been complaints about some features not being as accessible as they were before."

John made a note: "UI Upgrade - Dashboard, Navigation, Forms." He then asked, "And what about the backend integration? What did that involve?"

"The backend integration was more complex," Systems Sarah explained. "We migrated to a new database system, optimized data retrieval processes, and implemented new security protocols. This was supposed to streamline operations, but it seems to have introduced some unforeseen issues."

John wrote: "Backend Integration - New Database, Data Retrieval, Security Protocols." He stepped back to look at the whiteboard. "Alright, we need to consider how these changes might have impacted user experience and system performance. Have we received specific types of complaints that we can categorize?"

Systems Sarah nodded, "Yes, the tickets generally fall into three categories: usability issues, performance slowdowns, and data discrepancies."

John added these categories to the whiteboard. "Usability, Performance, Data Discrepancies. This gives us a framework to start our analysis. We'll need to look at the nature of these tickets more closely and see if we can trace them back to specific elements of the upgrades."

He paused, tapping the marker against the board. "We'll also need to check the timing of these complaints to see if there's a clear spike following the upgrades. This could help us pinpoint the exact issues."

Systems Sarah agreed, "That makes sense. We should also review any feedback we received during the beta testing phase of these upgrades. There might be some clues there."

John smiled, feeling a sense of direction. "Great idea. Let's gather all this data and reconvene tomorrow to start our deep dive. We'll get to the bottom of this."

With their plan set, John felt invigorated. The potential to solve this problem not only promised a significant reduction in support tickets but also offered him a renewed sense of purpose and clarity in his professional journey.

Identify the Solutions

The following morning, John arrived at the office with a sense of determination. He felt the excitement of tackling a complex problem with the potential to make a significant impact. After grabbing a quick coffee, he headed to the meeting room where Sarah and Peter were already setting up.

"Good morning, everyone," John greeted as he set his laptop on the table. "Let's get started. Sarah, do you have the data on the tickets and feedback from the beta testing?"

Systems Sarah nodded and connected her laptop to the projector. "Yes, I pulled together a detailed report. Here are the ticket counts by category over the past six months, with annotations for when the upgrades were implemented."

John studied the chart on the screen. It was clear that there was a noticeable spike in tickets shortly after each upgrade. He pointed to the first spike. "This corresponds to the UI upgrade. Let's dig into the usability issues first. What specific complaints did we receive?"

Systems Sarah brought up a spreadsheet detailing the usability tickets. "Most of the complaints were about the new navigation features. Users found them confusing compared to the old system. There were also several issues with the redesigned dashboard – some features were harder to find, and a few reports were missing."

John made notes on the whiteboard. "Navigation confusion, missing reports, difficult features. Okay, let's look at the performance issues next. These started spiking after the backend integration, right?"

Process Peters chimed in, "Yes, exactly. Users have been experiencing slow load times, particularly when accessing large data sets. There have also been intermittent crashes that we can't consistently replicate."

John added to the whiteboard: "Performance - Slow load times, intermittent crashes." He then asked, "What about the data discrepancies?"

Systems Sarah clicked to the next section of the report. "This has been the most alarming. Users reported that some data entries were missing or incorrect. It seems to affect records that were migrated from the old database to the new one."

John's brow furrowed. "Data integrity issues can be critical. This might explain why these two upgrades had such a significant impact on support ticket volumes."

Process Peters nodded in agreement. "Indeed, the data discrepancies are particularly concerning. If users can't trust the data, it undermines the entire system."

John paused to organize his thoughts. "Alright, we have a clear direction. Let's break into teams and tackle these issues systematically. Sarah, can you please lead the effort on the UI issues? Work with the design team to see how we can simplify the navigation and restore any missing reports."

Systems Sarah agreed. "Absolutely, I'll get started on that right away."

John turned to Process Peters. "Can you please focus on the performance issues? Look into the backend integration, especially the data retrieval processes. Let's identify what's causing the slowdowns and crashes."

Process Peters nodded. "Consider it done. I'll coordinate with the infrastructure team."

"I'll take the lead on the data discrepancies," John continued. "I'll review the migration logs and compare the data before and after the transition. We need to ensure our data integrity is restored."

With their tasks assigned, the team set to work. Over the next few days, John delved into the data migration logs, tracing each step of the process to identify where things might have gone wrong. Systems Sarah collaborated with the design team, conducting user feedback sessions to pinpoint the pain points in the new UI. Process Peters coordinated with the infrastructure team to analyze the backend processes, running stress tests to replicate the performance issues.

By the end of the week, they regrouped to share their findings. Systems Sarah reported first. "We've identified several areas in the navigation that need to be more intuitive. We're working on updates to make these features easier to find and use. The missing reports were a result of some overlooked dependencies during the redesign, and we're in the process of restoring them."

Process Peters followed. "We pinpointed the performance bottlenecks to a few inefficient queries in the new database. Optimizing these queries has already improved load times. We're also addressing the intermittent crashes, which seem to be related to memory leaks in the new integration layer."

John concluded with his findings. "The data discrepancies were due to some corrupted records during the migration. We've identified the corrupted batches and are in the process of correcting them. Additionally, we've put checks in place to prevent future occurrences."

With the issues identified and solutions underway, the team felt a renewed sense of accomplishment.

They knew there was still work to be done, but the path forward was clear. John's curiosity and systematic approach had not only helped solve the immediate problem but also reinvigorated his passion for his work. This experience reminded him why he loved being a business analyst and gave him a clearer sense of his professional identity.

As they wrapped up, John looked around at his colleagues. "Great work, everyone. This has been a challenging few weeks, but we've made significant progress. Let's keep the momentum going and ensure we deliver a more stable and user-friendly system."

Systems Sarah and Process Peters both smiled, feeling the same sense of achievement. "Agreed," said Systems Sarah. "Let's do this."

As John left the office that evening, he felt a sense of clarity and purpose that had been missing for a while. He realized that it wasn't about mastering every discipline perfectly but about using his curiosity and problem-solving skills to make a meaningful impact. And that was exactly what he planned to do moving forward.

Problem Solver Extraordinaire

As the weeks went by, the team's efforts started to bear fruit. The user interface became more intuitive, performance improved dramatically, and the data discrepancies were resolved. The number of support tickets began to drop, much to the relief of the entire support team.

One afternoon, Systems Sarah and Process Peters decided to take a moment to reflect on their progress and acknowledge the hard work that had been put in. They agreed to meet in the same meeting room where this journey had begun, and they invited John to join them.

John entered the meeting room, noticing the relaxed and satisfied expressions on Systems Sarah and Process Peter's faces. "Hey, what's up?" he asked, curious about the informal meeting.

Systems Sarah smiled warmly. "We wanted to take a moment to acknowledge all the hard work that's been done over the past few weeks. And, more importantly, to thank you for your incredible problem-solving skills."

Process Peters nodded in agreement. "John, your ability to dissect complex issues, identify root causes, and come up with practical solutions is truly remarkable. We were feeling quite overwhelmed when the ticket numbers started to rise, but you brought a sense of clarity and direction that was desperately needed."

John felt a wave of gratitude and humility. "Thank you, both. It was definitely a team effort, though. Everyone played a crucial role in turning things around."

"Absolutely," Systems Sarah agreed. "But we couldn't have done it without your leadership and analytical mindset. Your skill in breaking down the problem into manageable parts and guiding us through each step was invaluable. It's clear that problem-solving is your key strength."

Process Peters added, "You have a knack for seeing the bigger picture while also understanding the details. That's not something you see every day. It's a strength that sets you apart and one that's incredibly valuable in our line of work."

John's face lit up with a smile. He had always been his own harshest critic, constantly striving for improvement and often questioning his abilities. Hearing this acknowledgment from his peers was both uplifting and validating.

"Thank you, both. It means a lot to hear that," John said, his voice filled with gratitude. "I've always believed in the power of collaboration and learning from each other. This project has been a testament to that."

Systems Sarah nodded. "And you've taught us a lot in the process. Your approach to problem-solving has inspired us to think differently and tackle challenges head-on."

Process Peters looked at John with admiration. "You know, John, if I had to define you professionally in a few words, I'd say you're a 'Problem Solver Extraordinaire.'"

They all laughed, the tension of the past few weeks melting away in the light-hearted moment.

John felt a renewed sense of purpose and direction. He realized that while he might never master every discipline, his strength lay in his ability to analyze, solve problems, and guide his team through challenges. This clarity brought him closer to understanding his true calling.

As they wrapped up the meeting, Systems Sarah and Process Peters both reached for another hot jam donut, continuing the small ritual that had started this journey. John looked at them and felt a deep sense of camaraderie and fulfillment. He knew that whatever challenges lay ahead, he had the skills and the support of his team to face them head-on.

"Here's to many more challenges and even more solutions," John said, raising his donut in a toast.

"Cheers to that," Systems Sarah and Process Peters echoed, their spirits high as they looked forward to the future.

John walked out of the meeting room with a spring in his step, ready to embrace whatever came next. He was confident in his abilities and grateful for the journey that had led him to this moment. And for the first time in a long time, he felt truly enlightened.

Chapter 08

The New Establishment

As John walked out of the meeting room, a newfound sense of clarity and purpose washed over him. He had always enjoyed solving problems, but now he realized it was his true calling. He wanted to explore opportunities where he could focus on this passion without being confined by a specific role or title.

Over the next few days, John reflected on his career and the various projects he had worked on. He had thrived in environments where he could tackle complex problems, devise innovative solutions, and lead his team to success. He began to research potential career paths that would allow him to leverage these skills.

One evening, while scrolling through a career website, John came across a listing for a freelance consultant specializing in business analysis and problem-solving. The job description resonated with him: providing expert advice to companies facing operational challenges, implementing strategic solutions, and ensuring successful project outcomes. The flexibility of freelance work appealed to him, offering the chance to work on diverse projects and industries without being tied down to a single role or organization.

Excited by the prospect, John decided to reach out to a few freelance consultants he found online. He arranged coffee meetings with them to learn more about their experiences and the realities of freelance work. He also discussed the idea with Systems Sarah and Process Peters, seeking their advice and perspective.

"That's a fantastic idea, John," Systems Sarah said during one of their catch-up meetings. "You have a natural talent for problem-solving, and as a freelance consultant, you could make a significant impact on multiple businesses. Plus, it would give you the freedom to choose projects that truly excite you."

Process Peters nodded in agreement. "I think it's a great fit for you. You're not someone who likes to be confined to a single role. Freelancing would allow you to keep learning, growing, and tackling new challenges constantly."

Buoyed by their support, John decided to take the plunge. He updated his LinkedIn profile, highlighting his problem-solving expertise and his interest in freelance consulting. He also revamped his resume and began applying for freelance opportunities.

Laying the Foundation for the Path Ahead

John's journey into the freelancing world began long before he officially took the plunge. It was a series of deliberate steps, reflective self-assessment, and strategic planning that set the stage for his transition. John had always been an analytical thinker with a knack for solving complex problems. Through his self-assessment exercise, he realized that his true calling lay in problem-solving. He had extensive experience in process analysis, systems integration, and data management, which he decided would be his primary areas of focus as a consultant. To ensure he was well-prepared, John started honing his skills:

Professional Development:

John's first step was a thorough self-assessment. He took stock of his skills, strengths, and areas of expertise, particularly focusing on problem-solving, which he realized was his true calling. He evaluated his experiences in process, system, and data analysis, identifying where he excelled and where he needed improvement. This self-awareness gave him a clear picture of what he could offer as a freelancer. He took advanced courses and earned certifications in business analysis, project management, and data analytics to bolster his credentials.

Portfolio Creation:

Understanding the importance of showcasing his skills, John began compiling a portfolio of his work. He included case studies of successful projects, detailed descriptions of the problems he solved, and testimonials from colleagues and clients. This portfolio would serve as a tangible proof of his capabilities and a key tool in attracting potential clients.

Building a Strong Professional Network

John knew that a strong professional network was crucial for a successful freelancing career. He started researching industry events, joining relevant online forums, and connecting with peers and mentors. He nurtured relationships with former colleagues, superiors, and clients, letting them know about his freelancing plans. These connections would become his initial sources of work and referrals.

Industry Events:

John attended conferences, seminars, and workshops related to his field. These events provided opportunities to meet potential clients and other freelancers, exchange ideas, and stay updated on industry trends. His presence at these events not only expanded his network but also positioned him as an engaged and knowledgeable professional.

LinkedIn:

Recognizing the power of social media, John optimized his LinkedIn profile. He connected with colleagues, industry leaders, and potential clients. Regularly sharing insights and articles, John demonstrated his thought leadership and kept his network engaged. His active presence on LinkedIn helped him stay top of mind for opportunities and collaborations.

By focusing on these strategies, John significantly expanded his professional network, laying a solid foundation for his freelancing career.

Setting Up the Business Infrastructure

After conducting thorough research and consulting with an accountant, John made the strategic decision to establish his consultancy as a Limited Liability Company (LLC). This choice was informed by a variety of factors carefully weighed against his business goals and needs.

Through his consultations, John gained valuable insights into the legal and financial implications of different business structures. He learned that forming an LLC would provide him with a clear separation between his personal and business finances, shielding his personal assets from any potential liabilities arising from his consulting work. This protection was particularly important to John, as it offered him peace of mind while venturing into the unpredictable terrain of freelance consulting.

Furthermore, John's accountant helped him understand the tax advantages and administrative requirements associated with an LLC. By carefully considering these factors and weighing them against his long-term objectives, John felt confident that this legal structure would best serve his interests and aspirations as a consultant.

In addition to seeking professional advice, John conducted extensive research on his own, delving into the intricacies of various business entities and their implications. This proactive approach allowed him to familiarize himself with the nuances of business formation and make informed decisions about his consultancy's structure.

By combining expert guidance with diligent research, John ensured that his choice of business entity aligned closely with his vision for his consultancy. This meticulous approach underscored his commitment to building a strong foundation for his business, setting the stage for future growth and success.

Recognizing the importance of protecting his business against potential legal claims, John also sought guidance from a registered insurance agent. After consulting with the agent and conducting market research, John made the strategic decision to purchase public liability and professional indemnity insurances.

This insurance coverage offered comprehensive protection against claims alleging errors, omissions, or negligence in the professional services he provided. By obtaining this coverage, John fortified his consultancy against the financial repercussions of any unforeseen challenges or disputes that might arise during client engagements.

Furthermore, John's decision to invest in public liability and professional indemnity insurance was informed by thorough market research and an understanding of industry standards and best practices. Through his research, he identified the common risks and liabilities faced by freelance consultants in his field, as well as the prevailing insurance coverage options available to mitigate these risks.

By leveraging insights from both his insurance agent and market research findings, John made a proactive and informed choice to prioritize risk management and safeguard his consultancy's financial stability and reputation. This strategic approach demonstrated his commitment to responsible business practices and positioned his consultancy for long-term success in a competitive marketplace.

In addition to consulting with legal and insurance professionals, John recognized the importance of seeking guidance from a business banker and accountant to establish a solid financial infrastructure for his consultancy.

John consulted with a business banker to set up a dedicated business bank account, a crucial step in keeping his personal and business finances separate. By opening a separate account for his consultancy, John ensured that his business transactions remained distinct from his personal expenses, simplifying accounting and tax reporting processes while enhancing financial transparency and credibility.

Furthermore, John engaged the services of an accountant to navigate the complexities of financial management and compliance. His accountant provided valuable insights and assistance in selecting and implementing accounting software tailored to his consultancy's needs. This software would enable John to streamline financial tasks such as invoicing, expense tracking, and budgeting, empowering him to efficiently manage his consultancy's finances while minimizing administrative burdens.

By proactively consulting with a business banker and accountant, John established a robust financial infrastructure that would support his consultancy's growth and success. Through their guidance and expertise, John gained the confidence and knowledge needed to navigate financial challenges effectively and focus on delivering exceptional value to his clients.

Creating an Online Presence

Recognizing the pivotal role of a robust online presence in today's digital landscape, John took proactive steps to establish his consultancy's visibility and credibility in the digital realm.

First and foremost, John understood that a professional website serves as the digital storefront for any business. Investing in the development of an aesthetically pleasing, user-friendly, and informative website was paramount. Collaborating closely with web designers and developers, John ensured that his website not only reflected the essence of his consultancy but also provided visitors with a seamless browsing experience. By detailing his services in process analysis, systems integration, and data management, John effectively showcased his expertise and experience to potential clients.

In addition to highlighting his services, John recognized the importance of thought leadership and expertise positioning in attracting and retaining clients. To this end, he integrated a blog section into his website, serving as a platform to share valuable insights, industry trends, and best practices. Through well-researched articles, case studies, and informative guides, John was geared to position himself as an authority in his field. By addressing pertinent pain points and offering practical solutions, he aimed to not only enhance his credibility but also engage visitors by fostering a sense of trust and rapport.

Furthermore, John's content marketing efforts were strategically aligned with his consultancy's objectives and target audience preferences. By consistently delivering high-quality content that resonated with his audience's interests and challenges, John aimed to attract organic traffic to his website, thereby augmenting his online visibility and expanding his reach within the industry.

Overall, John's approach to creating an online presence underscored his commitment to building a strong consultancy brand. Through meticulous website development and compelling content marketing initiatives, he aimed to effectively showcase his expertise, attract prospective clients, and position his consultancy for sustained growth and success in the competitive freelance consulting landscape.

Testing the Waters

With the foundation of his new establishment taking shape and solidifying, it was time for John to test the strength and durability of his consultancy.

Side Projects

John began by taking on small consulting projects during weekends and evenings. These side projects ranged from process audits for small businesses to data management solutions for local non-profits. Each project offered John practical experience, allowing him to apply his skills in real-world settings. This hands-on experience was invaluable, highlighting both his strengths and areas that needed improvement.

With every project, John meticulously documented his work, capturing the problems he addressed, the solutions he implemented, and the results achieved. This growing portfolio became a powerful tool, demonstrating his expertise and track record to potential clients. The additional income from these side projects provided financial stability, easing the transition from a salaried job to freelancing and allowing him to invest in necessary tools and resources for his consultancy.

Working on various projects helped John refine his consulting approach. He experimented with different methodologies and techniques, discovering what worked best for different types of clients and projects.

Feedback Loop

Understanding the importance of continuous improvement, John actively sought feedback from his initial clients. After each project, he would ask for honest opinions about his work. This feedback was crucial in identifying his strengths and areas where he could improve. Positive feedback reinforced his confidence, while constructive criticism provided valuable insights into areas needing enhancement.

By acting on the feedback received, John fine-tuned his services. For instance, when a client mentioned that his communication could be clearer, he worked on improving his communication skills for future projects. This iterative process of receiving feedback and making adjustments ensured that his services were always evolving and improving.

Effective client interaction is key to successful consulting. Feedback on his interaction skills helped John become more attuned to client needs, preferences, and expectations. He learned how to manage client relationships better, set clear expectations, and ensure client satisfaction. Asking for feedback demonstrated to clients that John valued their opinions and was committed to providing the best possible service. This practice built trust and stronger relationships with his clients, leading to repeat business and referrals.

Building Confidence

By taking on side projects and actively seeking feedback, John built a solid foundation for his freelance career. These steps provided practical experience and financial stability, helping him refine his skills, build a portfolio, and establish strong client relationships. This careful and strategic approach ensured that when he finally transitioned to full-time freelancing, he will be well-prepared to navigate the challenges and opportunities that lay ahead.

John's meticulous approach to testing the waters paid off, laying the groundwork for a successful freelance consulting career. He was ready to face the future with confidence, knowing that his preparation had set him up for success.

Taking the Plunge

John knew that financial stability was crucial during the initial phase of his freelancing journey. To provide a financial safety net, he meticulously saved enough money to cover at least six months of living expenses. This savings cushion gave him the confidence to leave his salaried job, knowing he had the means to support himself while building his client base and securing steady work.

For several months, John diligently tracked his expenses, identified areas where he could cut costs, and saved aggressively. He created a detailed budget that accounted for rent, utilities, groceries, insurance, and other essential expenses. By living frugally and prioritizing his savings, John gradually built a substantial financial buffer.

This savings cushion served as a safety net, allowing him to focus on establishing his freelancing business without the constant worry of financial strain. Knowing he had enough funds to cover his living expenses for six months provided John with the peace of mind needed to take calculated risks and fully commit to his new venture.

The next task for John was understanding the risks of income instability. To mitigate this risk, John started focusing on building a reliable client pipeline before making the full switch to freelancing. He aimed to secure a few longer-term contracts that would provide a steady stream of income during the transition period.

John leveraged his professional network, reaching out to former colleagues, industry contacts, and initial clients who had been satisfied with his side projects. He communicated his availability for long-term engagements and highlighted his expertise in process analysis, systems integration, and data management. By showcasing his successful track record and the value he could bring to their projects, John was able to establish a pipeline of potential contracts that would sustain him during the early months of his freelancing journey.

He also joined freelancing platforms and industry-specific forums to identify potential clients and opportunities. By actively participating in discussions, sharing his insights, and offering advice, John continued building upon his reputation of a knowledgeable and reliable consultant.

Feeling prepared and supported, John finally decided to take the plunge into full-time freelancing. He tendered his resignation from his current role with a mix of excitement and apprehension. Understanding the importance of maintaining professional relationships, he made sure to leave on good terms.

John scheduled a meeting with his manager to discuss his decision. In the meeting, he expressed heartfelt gratitude for the opportunities and experiences he had gained during his tenure. He highlighted specific projects and mentorship moments that had significantly contributed to his professional growth. By providing adequate notice and offering to assist with the transition, John ensured that his departure would be smooth and amicable.

His manager appreciated John's transparency and professionalism. They discussed a transition plan, ensuring that John's responsibilities would be adequately covered. John offered to train his replacement and make himself available for any questions even after his departure, demonstrating his commitment to the team's success.

News of John's resignation spread through the office, and his colleagues approached him with mixed feelings. They were sad to see him go but also excited for his new venture. Many expressed their support, sharing words of encouragement and wishing him success in his new journey. Some colleagues shared stories of their own entrepreneurial dreams, finding inspiration in John's decision to pursue freelancing.

Several superiors and peers offered to stay in touch and provide referrals or collaboration opportunities in the future. They recognized John's talent and dedication, and they wanted to continue their professional relationship. This positive exit not only preserved his professional network but also opened doors for potential future engagements.

John felt a sense of relief and anticipation as he wrapped up his final weeks. He meticulously documented his ongoing projects, ensuring that his successor would have all the necessary information to take over seamlessly. He also spent time reflecting on his journey within the company, appreciating the skills and knowledge he had acquired.

Farewell

As his last day approached, the company organized a small farewell gathering. John was touched by the gesture, as colleagues shared memories and expressed their appreciation for his contributions. It was a bittersweet moment, but it reinforced his belief that he was making the right decision.

Having spent over seven years of his professional life at this company, John knew he couldn't leave without catching up with the people who had helped shape his career. With only a few days left before his departure, he began organizing meetups with his most trusted colleagues. The first on his list was Process Peters.

John and Process Peters met for lunch at their favorite cafe, a place where they had often brainstormed ideas and shared countless professional insights. The familiarity of the surroundings brought a sense of comfort to John as he prepared for an emotional conversation.

As they sat down, the aroma of freshly brewed coffee filled the air, and John couldn't help but feel nostalgic. "John, I still can't believe you're leaving us." Said Process Peters, "But I have to say, I'm incredibly proud of you for taking this step. Freelancing suits you—you've always had that entrepreneurial spark."

John gave him an appreciative nod and said, "Thanks, Peter. You've been such a great mentor. I learned so much from you about process optimization and project management. I couldn't have asked for a better guide during these years."

Process Peters took a sip of his coffee and leaned back, with a look of genuine pride on his face he said, "It's been a pleasure working with you, John. You're meticulous, dedicated, and a quick learner. Those qualities will serve you well in your new venture. Just remember, if you ever need advice or just want to chat, I'm just a phone call away."

John nodded, feeling a mixture of gratitude and sadness. "I appreciate that, Peter. And I'll definitely take you up on that. Your support means a lot to me."

They continued their conversation, reminiscing about past projects and the challenges they had overcome together. Process Peters recounted a particularly tough project where John's innovative thinking had saved the day, and they both laughed at the memory of late-night work sessions fueled by caffeine, donuts, and determination.

That evening, John met Systems Sarah at a local bar they both frequented after work. The place was buzzing with energy, filled with the hum of conversations and clinking glasses. They managed to find a quiet corner to sit and talk, away from the lively crowd.

As they settled in, Systems Sarah raised her glass with a warm smile. "Here's to you, John. You're going to do great things out there. I'm really excited for you."

They clinked glasses, and John felt a sense of relief as the weight of the day's emotions started to lift. He took a sip of his drink and smiled back at Systems Sarah. "Thanks, Sarah. You've been an inspiration to me. Your expertise in systems integration and your leadership style are things I've always admired and tried to emulate."

Systems Sarah took a thoughtful sip of her drink, her eyes reflecting the memories they shared. "You've got a knack for systems analysis, John. Remember the time we pulled that all-nighter to debug that critical system error? You kept your cool and found the solution. That's when I knew you were destined for bigger things."

John chuckled, the memory of that intense but rewarding experience coming back to him vividly. "Yeah, that was a tough night, but we got through it together. I'm going to miss our late-night problem-solving sessions. You've taught me so much about resilience and technical prowess."

Systems Sarah nodded, her eyes reflecting a mix of pride and affection. "And don't forget the importance of balance. Make sure to take breaks and enjoy the freelancing lifestyle. It's about freedom, after all."

John nodded thoughtfully. "You're right, Sarah. It's easy to get caught up in the work, but I'm looking forward to finding that balance. Freelancing is a big step, but it feels like the right move."

Systems Sarah reached across the table and placed a reassuring hand on John's arm. "You'll do great, John. Just remember to stay true to yourself and your values. And if you ever need advice or just want to chat, you know where to find me."

John felt a surge of gratitude for Systems Sarah's unwavering support. "Thank you, Sarah. Your support means the world to me. I'll definitely keep in touch."

They spent the rest of the evening reminiscing about the projects they had worked on together, the challenges they had overcome, and the lessons they had learned along the way. As they laughed and shared stories, John felt a deep sense of appreciation for the mentorship and friendship Systems Sarah had provided.

As the night drew to a close, John and Systems Sarah stood up to leave. They hugged, knowing that while this was the end of their daily interactions, it was not the end of their connection. John walked away from the bar feeling both nostalgic and excited for the future, ready to embrace the new challenges and opportunities that freelancing would bring.

The next day, John caught up with Data David over coffee. They met at their favorite cozy coffee shop, a spot that had become their go-to place for impromptu data discussions and brainstorming sessions. The aroma of freshly brewed coffee filled the air as they settled into their usual corner table.

Data David: "John, your decision to move into freelancing is bold, but knowing you, it's the right one. You've always had a way with data that few can match."

John felt a surge of pride hearing this from someone he respected so much. He took a moment to absorb the compliment before responding.

John: "Thanks, David. Working with you has been one of the highlights of my career here. Your analytical skills and the way you approach data problems have taught me a lot."

David smiled, reminiscing about their many collaborations. "Remember that data migration project? We were up against the clock, but you handled the pressure like a pro. Those are the kind of skills that will make you a fantastic consultant."

John nodded, appreciating the acknowledgment. "That project was intense, but we nailed it. I learned so much from that experience. I'm going to miss our data deep-dives and those moments of breakthrough."

David raised his coffee cup in a toast. "Just keep being curious and meticulous. Those qualities will carry you far. And don't hesitate to reach out if you need a hand with any data-related challenges."

They clinked their coffee cups together, and John felt a wave of nostalgia mixed with excitement for the future.

John: "You know, David, those late-night sessions, crunching numbers and making sense of all that data, are some of my favorite memories. We pushed each other to think differently and come up with innovative solutions. I'm really going to miss that dynamic."

Data David leaned back, his expression thoughtful. "It's not just the data work I'll miss, but the way we challenged each other intellectually. You have this way of seeing patterns and connections that others often miss. It's been inspiring to watch you grow."

John chuckled. "And you've taught me the importance of thoroughness and patience. You always say that the devil is in the details, and it's something I've come to appreciate deeply. Your meticulous nature has definitely rubbed off on me."

The conversation flowed easily as they reminisced about past projects and the lessons learned along the way. They shared stories of late nights and early mornings, of the thrill of finding solutions and the camaraderie that came with working through tough challenges together.

Data David: "You know, John, freelancing is going to suit you well. You'll have the freedom to explore different projects and industries. And with your skill set, you'll be in high demand. Just remember, the key to success is not just in the work you do, but in the relationships you build."

John nodded, taking David's words to heart. "I've always admired how you maintain strong relationships with clients and colleagues. It's something I'm going to focus on in my freelancing career. Building trust and delivering consistent results."

Data David smiled, raising his cup once more. "To new beginnings and continued success. You've got this, John."

They toasted again, the clink of their cups signaling not just an end but a new beginning. John felt a renewed sense of confidence and gratitude. As they finished their coffee, they made plans to stay in touch and continue sharing their insights and experiences.

Leaving the coffee shop, John reflected on the conversation. The support and encouragement from Data David reaffirmed his decision to step into the world of freelancing. He was ready to tackle new challenges and seize new opportunities, armed with the knowledge and skills he had honed over the years.

The day finally arrived. It was John's last working day at the company he had called home for over seven years. His colleagues had organized an informal lunch as a sendoff for him, gathering the entire team, both past and present. This included Process Peters, Systems Sarah, Data David, and other colleagues he had worked with closely. They chose a cozy restaurant near the office, a familiar place filled with warmth and camaraderie.

As everyone settled in, the atmosphere was a mix of celebration and nostalgia. Laughter and chatter filled the room as they reminisced about shared experiences and memorable projects.

John stood up, raising his glass. "I wanted to thank each and every one of you for making these past seven years so memorable. I've learned so much from all of you, and your support has been incredible."

Colleague 1: "John, it's been great working with you. Your dedication and problem-solving skills are unmatched. We're going to miss you."

Colleague 2: "You always brought a unique perspective to our projects. Your insights and hard work made a big difference."

John smiled, feeling a wave of emotion. "Thank you, everyone. I'm going to miss our collaborative spirit and the way we tackled challenges together. But I'm excited about this new chapter, and I hope to keep in touch with all of you."

Process Peters: "John, you've been an asset to this team. We wish you all the best in your freelancing journey. Don't be a stranger."

Systems Sarah: "And remember, our doors are always open for collaboration. We're excited to see where your new path takes you."

Data David: "Good luck, John. You've got this."

The room echoed with applause and cheers. Stories were shared, each one highlighting John's contributions and the unique mark he had left on the team. They laughed about late-night work sessions, celebrated project successes, and even fondly remembered the challenges that had brought them closer together.

John felt a mixture of pride and sadness. These were not just colleagues but friends who had become like family over the years. The support and encouragement he received reaffirmed his decision to step into the world of freelancing. He was ready to tackle new challenges and seize new opportunities, knowing that he carried with him the skills, experiences, and friendships he had built.

As the lunch drew to a close, John exchanged heartfelt goodbyes with each person. There were promises to stay in touch, to meet up, and to collaborate in the future. He left the restaurant feeling both nostalgic and excited about his future.

Walking back to the office one last time, John reflected on his journey. The support and encouragement from his colleagues had given him the confidence to embrace the unknown. His heart was full of gratitude, and his mind was set on the new adventures that awaited him in the world of freelancing. He was ready to face whatever challenges came his way, buoyed by the memories of the past seven years and the friendships that would continue to inspire him.

Chapter 09

Full Speed Ahead

John woke up on the Monday following his farewell and departure from the old company. He went through his morning routine as usual—brushing his teeth, making breakfast, and getting dressed for the day. But as he finished tying his shoes, a realization hit him like a ton of bricks: "I don't have an office to go to."

The revelation was both daunting and freeing at the same time. The familiar rhythm of heading to the office, chatting with colleagues, and diving into the day's tasks was gone. Instead, he was now faced with the exhilarating challenge of building his own venture from scratch. The thought of being his own boss filled him with a mixture of excitement and anxiety.

John took a deep breath, reminding himself that he had planned for this moment. He had saved up a financial buffer for six months, ensuring that he wouldn't need to worry about money in the short term. This safety net gave him the freedom to focus on establishing his freelancing business without the immediate pressure of financial constraints.

With a sense of renewal and a mission to achieve his newfound goals, John walked into his study. This room, which had always served as a quiet space for reading and occasional work-from-home days, was now his official workspace. He sat down at his desk and opened his personal laptop, which had transformed into his work laptop. The first task was clear: build a pipeline of work to keep himself busy and manage his expenses.

John's study was well-organized, with a large desk, a comfortable chair, and a window that let in plenty of natural light. He had already set up a whiteboard on one wall, ready to capture ideas and plans. On his desk, he had his planner, a cup of freshly brewed coffee, and a stack of business cards he had collected over the years.

He began by reviewing his list of contacts and potential clients. Over the past few months, he had networked extensively, attended industry events, and reached out to former colleagues and clients to let them know about his new venture. Now it was time to follow up and see which of these connections could lead to his first few projects.

John drafted personalized emails to his contacts, reminding them of his skills and experience, and expressing his eagerness to collaborate on future projects. He tailored each message to highlight how his expertise could address their specific needs and challenges.

Next, he updated his LinkedIn profile to reflect his new status as a freelance consultant. He shared a post announcing his career shift, outlining the services he offered, and inviting his network to reach out for consultations. Within minutes, he received several likes and comments from supportive colleagues, wishing him luck and offering to refer him to potential clients.

Feeling a surge of motivation, John started brainstorming content for his blog. He had always wanted to share his insights and experiences in process analysis, systems integration, and data management. This blog would not only establish him as a thought leader but also attract potential clients to his website.

As he sipped his coffee, John outlined his first few blog posts. He decided to write about common pitfalls in systems integration and how to avoid them, drawing on his extensive experience to provide practical advice. He also planned a series of case studies showcasing successful projects he had worked on, highlighting the value he brought to his clients.

By the end of the day, John had sent out several emails, updated his online presence, and drafted his first blog post. It was a productive start, and he felt a sense of accomplishment. The initial uncertainty had given way to a clear plan of action, and he was ready to embrace the challenges of freelancing.

As the sun set and the room grew dim, John leaned back in his chair and smiled. The journey ahead was uncharted, but he felt prepared and determined. With his skills, experience, and a solid plan, he was confident that he could build a successful freelancing business. The freedom and responsibility of being his own boss were now his reality, and he was ready to make the most of it.

Early Days

As John continued his daily routine of sending emails to his contacts and following up with some of his past clients, his efforts began to bear fruit. Many of the clients he had previously assisted with smaller projects and assignments reached out to him with more substantial work opportunities. In the past, his availability had been limited due to his full-time job, preventing him from committing to larger projects. But now, with all the time in the world, he was ready to focus on bigger and better projects.

Within two weeks of quitting his old job, John managed to secure a project that would keep him busy for at least 2-3 months. It was a fantastic start, and John couldn't be happier. The project involved a comprehensive systems integration for a mid-sized company looking to streamline their operations. This was the kind of challenge John thrived on, and he was eager to dive in.

Starting the project in a full-time capacity meant that John now had to work at the client's office. The change of scenery was refreshing. He set up his workspace at the client's site, complete with his laptop, notebooks, and a small plant to add a personal touch. The office buzzed with activity, and John felt invigorated by the new environment.

On his first day at the client's office, John was introduced to the team he would be working with. They were a mix of IT professionals, business analysts, and project managers. John quickly realized that his role would not only be to deliver the technical aspects of the project but also to bridge the gap between the technical team and the business stakeholders.

As he settled into his new role, John organized a kick-off meeting to align everyone on the project goals and timelines. He presented his approach to systems integration, emphasizing the importance of clear communication and collaboration. The team responded positively, and John felt a surge of confidence.

The following weeks were a whirlwind of activity. John spent his days conducting meetings, analyzing existing systems, and mapping out the integration plan. He worked closely with the IT team to understand the technical challenges and collaborated with the business analysts to ensure that the integration met the company's strategic objectives.

Despite the demanding schedule, John found the work incredibly fulfilling. Each day brought new challenges and opportunities to learn. The client's team was supportive, and John appreciated their willingness to adapt and collaborate. He quickly became a valued member of the team, known for his problem-solving skills and his ability to simplify complex concepts.

John's evenings were often spent reflecting on the day's progress and planning for the next steps. He maintained a detailed project journal, documenting the decisions made and the lessons learned. This not only helped him stay organized but also served as a valuable resource for future projects.

The project progressed smoothly, and within a month, significant milestones were achieved. The integration plan was finalized, and the initial phases of implementation began. John's ability to manage the project efficiently and effectively impressed the client, and they expressed their satisfaction with his work.

As the project moved forward, John continued to receive inquiries from other potential clients. His reputation as a skilled and reliable consultant was growing, and he was excited about the possibilities that lay ahead. He realized that his decision to become a freelancer had opened up a world of opportunities that he had never imagined.

One evening, as John was packing up his things at the client's office, he paused to reflect on his journey so far. The transition from a full-time employee to a freelance consultant had been challenging, but it had also been incredibly rewarding. He felt a deep sense of satisfaction knowing that he was making a difference and doing what he loved.

With the project well underway and new opportunities on the horizon, John knew that he had made the right choice. He was ready to embrace the future with confidence and enthusiasm, knowing that the best was yet to come.

Teething Issues

John's current client was thoroughly impressed by his work and expressed interest in offering him more projects. However, due to internal budgeting and funding approval delays, they couldn't commit to anything immediately. At the same time, John was in dialogue with another potential client who wanted to engage his services for three months, starting within two weeks. This potential client was a large corporation with promising prospects, making the decision even more difficult.

John found himself at a crossroads. The current client was a repeat client, and maintaining a good relationship with them was crucial as they could be a source of ongoing work in the future. On the other hand, the new client represented a significant opportunity with a large corporation, potentially opening doors to even bigger projects and further establishing his reputation in the industry.

This was a challenge John had not anticipated in his planning. It was a good problem to have, indicating that his freelancing business was gaining traction. However, it also meant he had to make a tough choice. If only he had more people working with him, he could have managed both clients with ease. But, as a solo freelancer, he had to be realistic about his capabilities and time constraints.

John decided to tackle the situation from a business viewpoint. He started by evaluating both opportunities based on a few critical factors:

Relationship and Long-Term Potential

Current Client: A repeat client with a strong relationship established. Continuity with them could ensure steady work and income in the future.

New Client: A large corporation with significant potential for high-value projects. Establishing a relationship here could open doors to a new network and bigger opportunities.

Financial Considerations

Current Client: Although there was no immediate project, once their budgeting issues were resolved, they promised consistent work.

New Client: Offering a well-defined three-month engagement with a lucrative contract. The immediate financial benefits were clear.

Timing and Availability

Current Client: No immediate commitment, providing flexibility but uncertainty.

New Client: Required an immediate start, limiting flexibility but ensuring a defined workload and timeline.

Strategic Growth

Current Client: Ensuring ongoing projects could provide stability and gradual growth.

New Client: High-profile project with potential for rapid growth and expansion of his consultancy business.

After thoroughly weighing these factors, John decided to have an open conversation with both clients. He believed transparency and professionalism would help navigate this challenge effectively.

Conversation with the Current Client

John reached out to his contact at the current client's office.

John: "I wanted to thank you for considering me for future projects. I truly value our working relationship. However, I've been approached by another client with an immediate project that aligns with my skills and availability. Given your current budgeting delays, I was hoping to understand your timeline better. Is there a way we can schedule the upcoming projects around the new engagement I'm considering?"

The client appreciated John's honesty and professionalism. They explained their situation in more detail and acknowledged that they couldn't provide immediate work but were committed to future collaborations.

Conversation with the New Client

Next, John contacted the potential new client.

John: "Thank you for considering my services for your upcoming project. I'm excited about the opportunity to work with your team. However, I am currently wrapping up a project with another client and need to ensure a smooth transition. Could we discuss a slightly flexible start date, or would there be scope for a phased start where I can ramp up my involvement over the first few weeks?"

The new client was open to discussing the start date and appreciated John's proactive approach. They agreed to a phased start, allowing John to complete his current commitments while gradually ramping up his involvement with their project.

Resolution

By addressing both clients transparently, John was able to secure a phased start with the new client while maintaining a good relationship with the current client. He also began considering expanding his consultancy to include additional freelancers or subcontractors in the future. This would allow him to take on multiple projects simultaneously without compromising on quality or delivery.

In the end, John's approach not only resolved the immediate scheduling conflict but also set the stage for strategic growth in his freelancing career. He learned the importance of clear communication, flexibility, and strategic planning in managing client relationships and workload effectively. This experience also reinforced his belief in the value of transparency and professionalism, which would continue to guide him as he navigated the world of freelancing.

Joining Forces

It had been nearly three months since John quit his job and started working as a freelancer. He was wrapping up his first project as a freelancer and preparing to transition into another project for a large corporation. Since it was a phased transition, he started with four days a week at the old client's office and one day a week at the new client's office. Each week, John would work one less day for the old client and one extra day for the new client until he could dedicate all five days to the new client. The total transition duration was roughly a month.

As part of his onboarding process with the new client, John was scheduled to meet with one of the client's representatives at their head office. Being a punctual professional, John arrived at the client location ten minutes early. He signed in at the reception and sat on a couch in the waiting area, scrolling through his smartphone and reading business news.

Suddenly, he heard someone call his name. "John?" He looked up and felt something he had never felt before— butterflies in his stomach. Standing in front of him was a beautiful young woman, sharply dressed in professional attire with a gorgeous smile on her face and her hand extended for a handshake. John felt shy and nervous, momentarily forgetting where he was. He grabbed her hand awkwardly and shook it, his nervousness making his grip a bit too firm. The woman could sense his nervousness and said with a smile, "First day at the head office of a large corporation always makes you feel like an intern, doesn't it?"

John smiled awkwardly and nodded in agreement. "Well, my name is Shaveta and I am one of the freelance consultants working on the project you will be involved in. The leadership team thought it would be ideal if I gave you the induction and briefed you on the work we have been doing and the plans for the project moving forward."

John felt a wave of relief wash over him. "Nice to meet you, Shaveta," he said, trying to steady his voice. "I appreciate you taking the time to help me get up to speed."

Shaveta led John through the modern, bustling office to a conference room. Along the way, she pointed out key areas of the office, including the break room, the project management offices, and the IT support desk. John took mental notes, impressed by the scale and organization of the company.

Once they were seated in the conference room, Shaveta began the induction. She provided an overview of the project's scope, the objectives, and the current progress. "Our team has been working on integrating various systems to streamline the company's operations. We've made significant progress, but there are still some critical components that need to be addressed."

John listened intently, his initial nervousness fading as he immersed himself in the details of the project. Shaveta's clear explanations and insightful comments made it easy for him to grasp the current state of the project and understand the challenges ahead.

She handed John a detailed project plan, complete with timelines and key milestones. "Here's where we are now, and these are the targets we need to hit in the next few months. Your expertise in systems integration will be crucial for achieving these goals."

John reviewed the document, nodding thoughtfully. "This looks comprehensive. I'm excited to dive in and start contributing."

Shaveta smiled warmly. "We're glad to have you on board, John. Your reputation precedes you, and I'm confident you'll be a valuable asset to the team."

As they wrapped up the meeting, John felt a renewed sense of purpose and excitement. He was eager to tackle the challenges of this new project and prove himself in this new environment. The butterflies in his stomach had settled, replaced by a feeling of anticipation and determination.

Shaveta stood up and extended her hand again. "Welcome to the team, John. Let's make this project a success."

John shook her hand, this time with a confident grip. "Thank you, Shaveta. I'm looking forward to working with you and the rest of the team."

As he left the conference room and made his way back to his desk, John couldn't help but feel grateful for this new opportunity. The transition from his old job to freelancing had been challenging, but moments like this reaffirmed his decision.

The following week, John was scheduled to work at the new client's location for two days. He had coordinated his schedule with Shaveta, and they both agreed to be in the office on those days to ensure a smooth transition and effective collaboration. As John delved deeper into the project, he couldn't help but notice how comfortable he felt in Shaveta's company. She was smart, ambitious, pretty, and most importantly, a problem solver just like him.

Over the weeks, as John and Shaveta continued to achieve milestones for their common client, their professional bond grew stronger. They spent countless hours brainstorming, troubleshooting, and strategizing, forming a seamless partnership. With each passing day, John began to realize that he might have feelings for Shaveta. And maybe, just maybe, Shaveta felt the same way about him.

One day, after they had delivered a significant milestone for the client, Shaveta suggested they celebrate their win. "How about a couple of drinks to toast our success?" she proposed with a twinkle in her eye. John readily agreed, feeling a mix of excitement and nervousness.

Shaveta led the way to a cozy bar near the client's office, a place she frequented for its relaxed atmosphere and decent selection of beverages. As they entered, the familiar hum of soft music and the clinking of glasses greeted them. The bar was just as Shaveta had described—quiet and inviting.

They found a corner table and ordered their drinks. The mood was celebratory, and they both felt a sense of accomplishment. "Here's to another milestone achieved," Shaveta said, raising her glass. "And to many more to come," John added, clinking his glass against hers.

As they sipped their drinks, their conversation flowed effortlessly. They talked about their journey so far, the challenges they had overcome, and their plans for the future. The professional façade began to melt away, revealing glimpses of their personal lives and dreams.

John couldn't help but admire Shaveta's passion and dedication. "You know, working with you has been one of the highlights of this project," he confessed. "You have this incredible ability to see solutions where others see problems."

Shaveta smiled warmly. "I could say the same about you, John. You have a way of making even the toughest challenges seem manageable. It's been a pleasure working alongside you."

The conversation took a more personal turn as they shared stories from their past and talked about their interests outside of work. John found himself drawn to Shaveta's laughter, her enthusiasm, and the way her eyes lit up when she talked about things she was passionate about.

As the evening progressed, John felt a growing connection between them. He decided to take a chance. "Shaveta, I know this might sound a bit forward, but I really enjoy spending time with you. Outside of work, I mean. Would you like to maybe grab dinner sometime, just the two of us?"

Shaveta looked at him, her smile widening. "I'd like that, John. I was hoping you'd ask."

Relieved and thrilled, John grinned. "Great. How about this weekend?"

"It's a date," Shaveta replied, raising her glass once more.

They finished their drinks, basking in the newfound connection that extended beyond their professional relationship. As they left the bar, walking side by side under the city lights, John felt a sense of excitement and anticipation.

The weeks ahead were filled with promise—not just for their project, but for something more personal and meaningful. John had ventured into the freelancing world seeking professional growth, but he found something even more special along the way. As he looked at Shaveta, he couldn't help but feel grateful for the serendipitous turn his journey had taken.

Over the coming weeks, as their project was nearing its conclusion, John received an exciting call from his old client. Their budget had been approved, and they wanted to offer him another six months of work. Thrilled by the prospect, John couldn't wait to share the news with Shaveta.

When he did, her eyes lit up with genuine happiness for him. "That's fantastic news, John! Congratulations," she said, her smile as radiant as ever.

Feeling buoyed by her enthusiasm, John asked, "Do you have anything lined up after this project?"

Shaveta nodded. "Actually, yes. Another client of mine wants me to collaborate on a large project that could keep me busy for approximately twelve months."

John smiled in admiration. "That's amazing, Shaveta. You're incredible at what you do."

As they discussed their respective projects, an idea began to form in John's mind. "You know," he said slowly, "why don't we join forces? We're both good at what we do, and if we teamed up, we could take on more clients and larger projects. We might even have the chance to grow a team."

Shaveta's eyes widened with interest, but then a cautious look crossed her face. "I love the idea, John, but I need to think about it. I'm concerned that our personal relationship might become a hindrance down the line. I wouldn't want to jeopardize our careers or what we've built together personally."

John felt a pang of disappointment but nodded in understanding. "I appreciate your honesty, Shaveta. It's important to think this through carefully. I don't want to rush into anything that might complicate things for us."

That night, John found himself deep in thought. He reflected on Shaveta's concerns and the potential implications of mixing their personal and professional lives. He valued their relationship deeply and didn't want to do anything that might jeopardize it. At the same time, he couldn't shake the feeling that they could create something remarkable together.

The following day, as they met for their usual coffee break, John decided to share his thoughts. "Shaveta, I've been thinking about what you said. You're right; we need to be careful. But I also think we have a unique opportunity here. We both have skills that complement each other, and I believe we could build something amazing together. What if we start small? We could collaborate on a few projects and see how it goes before making any long-term commitments."

Shaveta took a sip of her coffee, considering his proposal. "I appreciate your perspective, John. Maybe starting small is the way to go. We can test the waters and see how well we work together in a business capacity without putting too much at risk."

Relieved, John smiled. "That sounds like a sensible plan. Let's take it one step at a time and see where it leads us."

With that, they decided to pursue a trial collaboration. They agreed to start with a joint project that would allow them to leverage their combined expertise without overcommitting. As they wrapped up their current project and moved into this new phase, both John and Shaveta felt a renewed sense of excitement.

Their first joint project came from a referral through Shaveta's network. It was a medium-sized systems integration task with a tight deadline. They quickly fell into a rhythm, each playing to their strengths. John handled the technical aspects, while Shaveta focused on stakeholder management and strategic planning. Their collaboration was seamless, and the project was completed ahead of schedule, much to the client's delight.

Through this experience, John and Shaveta learned a lot about their working dynamics. They realized that their personal relationship could, in fact, enhance their professional collaboration. Their communication was clear, their trust was solid, and they supported each other through challenges.

One evening, after a long day of work, they sat down together to review their progress. "I think we make a pretty great team," John said, looking at Shaveta with a smile.

Shaveta nodded; her eyes sparkling. "I agree. Maybe this could work after all. Let's take on a few more projects and see how things go. If it continues to work well, we can consider formalizing our partnership."

John felt a surge of optimism. "Sounds like a plan. Here's to our future collaborations."

As they clinked their coffee mugs together, John felt a sense of fulfillment. The path ahead was still uncertain, but he knew that with Shaveta by his side, both personally and professionally, they could navigate any challenge that came their way.

Chapter 10

Testing the Limits

As the days turned into weeks and weeks turned into months, John and Shaveta experienced a range of emotional ups and downs. Their personal expectations from each other grew, and these began to seep into their work schedules. It became increasingly challenging to separate their professional and personal lives.

One particularly difficult period occurred when Shaveta found herself without any projects for four weeks. Simultaneously, John's client was experiencing budget constraints and couldn't offer work for both of them. Shaveta, who suddenly had more free time, hoped to spend it with John. She envisioned going for walks, having casual or romantic dinners, and enjoying each other's company. However, John's workload remained intense. He spent long hours at work and, when he finally got home, he wanted to unwind and relax alone.

This disparity in their needs started to put a strain on their relationship. Shaveta felt neglected and lonely, while John felt pressured and misunderstood. Neither of them was at fault, but the situation was becoming untenable. They both realized that if things continued this way, their relationship might fall apart under the mounting stress.

One evening, after a particularly tense day, John and Shaveta sat down to have an honest conversation. They decided to tackle this issue together, leveraging their problem-solving skills to find a solution.

"John, I feel like we're drifting apart," Shaveta began, her voice tinged with sadness. "I know you're busy with work, but I really miss spending time with you. I don't want this to come between us."

John looked at her, his heart heavy. "I miss spending time with you too, Shaveta. It's just that work has been so demanding lately, and I end up exhausted. I'm sorry if it feels like I'm neglecting you."

Shaveta sighed, "I understand, John. It's just that when I didn't have any projects, I felt a bit lost and wanted more of your company. Maybe we can find a way to balance our time better?"

John nodded thoughtfully. "Absolutely. How about we create a schedule that ensures we get quality time together without compromising on our work commitments?"

They grabbed a notebook and started brainstorming ideas.

Vision Alignment

The first thing they decided to test was their vision—both professional and personal. They knew each other well enough by now, but it was important that they dug deeper and understood each other's long-term goals and aspirations.

Armed with a couple of notebooks and a bottle of wine, they settled into their cozy living room, ready to explore their future together.

John: "Alright, let's start with our professional visions. Where do you see yourself in five years, Shaveta?"

Shaveta: "In five years, I want to be leading large-scale projects, possibly running my own consultancy firm. I envision a team of talented individuals working together to solve complex problems. What about you?"

John: "I see myself working on innovative projects, possibly branching out into different industries. I want to be known for my problem-solving skills and contribute to cutting-edge developments. I also have a dream of mentoring young professionals and helping them navigate their careers."

Shaveta: "That's amazing, John. It sounds like we both have aspirations to grow and lead in our fields. How do you feel about the idea of potentially merging our visions and creating a joint consultancy?"

John: "I love the idea. I think we could create something powerful together. We complement each other's skills so well. But we also need to make sure we maintain our individual identities and passions within the business."

They both nodded, feeling a sense of alignment in their professional goals. Next, they moved on to their personal visions.

John: "Now, let's talk about our personal visions. What do you see for us in the next few years?"

Shaveta: "I want us to have a balanced life, where we can pursue our careers but also make time for each other. I see us traveling, exploring new places, and enjoying quality time together. I also think about starting a family someday. What about you?"

John: "I want the same. A life where we support each other's dreams but also have adventures together. I see us building a home, maybe even working on passion projects side by side. And yes, I'd love to start a family when the time is right."

The conversation flowed effortlessly as they delved into deeper aspects of their visions, from financial goals to lifestyle preferences, and even how they envisioned their social lives evolving.

By the end of the evening, they had a clearer understanding of each other's dreams and aspirations. They realized that their visions were not only compatible but also had the potential to be mutually reinforcing. They could build a life where their professional and personal goals coexisted harmoniously.

The next step was to create a plan to turn these visions into reality. They decided to break their goals down into actionable steps and timelines, ensuring that they stayed aligned and supported each other through the journey.

John: "I think the key to making this work is continuous communication and being flexible. Our visions might evolve, and we need to be ready to adapt."

Shaveta: "Absolutely. Let's make a pact to have these vision-setting sessions regularly, maybe every six months, to ensure we're on track and still aligned."

With a renewed sense of purpose and a solid plan in place, John and Shaveta felt more connected than ever. They knew that by understanding and supporting each other's visions, they could build a fulfilling life together, both professionally and personally.

Boundary Setting

The next day, John and Shaveta decided to set some boundaries—both professional and personal. They understood that appreciating each other's space was crucial for maintaining a healthy relationship and productive work dynamic.

They sat down at the kitchen table, armed with notepads and a clear intent to establish guidelines that would help them respect each other's individual needs and preferences.

John: "Alright, let's start with professional boundaries. It's important that we don't let work consume our entire relationship. How do you feel about setting specific work hours?"

Shaveta: "I agree. We should set specific times when we're available for work-related discussions. Outside of those hours, we focus on our personal lives. How about 9 AM to 6 PM for work, and after that, we don't talk about work unless it's urgent?"

John: "That sounds good. We should also have a rule about not bringing work stress into our personal time. If something is bothering us at work, we discuss it during our work hours or scheduled check-ins."

Shaveta: "Absolutely. And if we need to work late or on weekends, we should give each other a heads-up in advance. That way, we can plan our personal time accordingly."

They both nodded, feeling a sense of clarity about their professional boundaries. Next, they moved on to personal boundaries.

John: "Now, let's talk about personal boundaries. It's important that we respect each other's need for personal space and time. What do you think?"

Shaveta: "I agree. We should have dedicated 'me-time' where we can do our own thing—read a book, go for a walk, or just relax. It's important for our individual well-being."

John: "I like that. Maybe we can each have one evening a week where we do something on our own or with our friends. It's also important that we respect each other's hobbies and interests, even if they're different from our own."

Shaveta: "Yes, and let's make sure we communicate openly about our needs. If one of us feels overwhelmed or needs more space, we should feel comfortable expressing that without the other taking it personally."

They continued to discuss and jot down their thoughts, creating a list of boundaries that would help them navigate their shared and individual spaces:

List of Boundaries

- **Work Hours:** Dedicated work hours from 9 AM to 6 PM. No work discussions outside these hours unless urgent.

- **Work Stress:** Address work-related issues during work hours or scheduled check-ins. Avoid bringing work stress into personal time.

- **Advance Notice:** Notify each other in advance if work requires extra hours or weekend commitments.

- **Me-Time:** Each person gets one evening a week for personal activities or time with friends.

- **Respect Hobbies:** Support and respect each other's hobbies and interests.

- **Open Communication:** Communicate openly about personal needs for space or time without fear of misunderstanding.

By setting these boundaries, John and Shaveta hoped to create a balanced and respectful environment where they could thrive both individually and as a couple. They knew that boundaries would help them maintain a healthy relationship and prevent potential conflicts.

As they finished their discussion, John looked at Shaveta and said, "I'm glad we're doing this. Setting these boundaries shows that we respect and care for each other's well-being."

Shaveta smiled. "Me too, John. This will help us appreciate each other's space and make our time together even more special."

With their boundaries clearly defined, John and Shaveta felt more confident about their ability to manage both their professional and personal lives. They knew that by respecting these boundaries, they could support each other better and strengthen their relationship.

That evening, they celebrated their new understanding with a quiet dinner at home. They cooked together, laughed, and talked about their plans for the weekend. The sense of harmony and mutual respect made them feel even closer, reinforcing their belief that they could navigate any challenge as long as they worked together.

Conflict Resolution

John and Shaveta did not indulge in any further discussions for a few days, allowing themselves time to digest the details of their earlier sessions on vision and boundaries. However, they knew there were other aspects of their personal and professional lives they needed to explore. After nearly a week, they felt ready to tackle the next important area on their list: conflict resolution.

One evening, they settled into their living room, the atmosphere comfortable and familiar. They knew that addressing conflict resolution was crucial for maintaining a healthy relationship and a productive work dynamic.

John: "Alright, let's talk about how we can manage conflicts better. We've had a few disagreements in the past, but I think we can improve our approach. What do you think?"

Shaveta: "I agree. It's natural to have conflicts, but the key is to handle them constructively. I think we should establish some ground rules for when we disagree."

They began by reflecting on past conflicts and how they had managed—or mismanaged—them. This reflection helped them understand what strategies had worked and what had not. They decided to role-play some of those scenarios to get a more hands-on experience and practice what they were trying to preach. But before doing that, they had to establish some ground rules.

Ground Rules

- **Stay Calm:** Both agreed that the first step in managing conflicts was to stay calm. They would take a few deep breaths and avoid raising their voices or getting overly emotional.

- **Listen Actively:** They decided to listen to each other without interrupting, ensuring they fully understood the other person's perspective before responding. This would help them feel heard and valued. Ask if unsure about the meaning behind a statement.

- **Use "I" Statements:** They would use "I" statements to express their feelings and needs without sounding accusatory. For example, "I feel upset when..." instead of "You always...". This will allow them to focus on their own sentiments rather than laying blame on the other person.

- **Take Breaks if Needed:** If a discussion became too heated, they agreed to take a short break to cool down before continuing. This would prevent the situation from escalating. If either party cannot calm down quickly, leave the conversation for another day but make sure you close the loop and conclude the conversation later.

- **Seek Solutions Together:** They committed to working together to find a solution that satisfied both parties, rather than trying to "win" the argument. They would focus on collaboration rather than competition.

- **Do Not Bring in a Third Party:** They both believed that the fundamental idea behind conflict resolution was to resolve conflicts between themselves. They agreed that involving a third party for mediation could escalate things unnecessarily and complicate their personal and professional relationship. If the situation ever boiled down to needing a third party, it would signal deeper, more serious concerns that needed addressing.

- **Apologize and Forgive:** They emphasized the importance of apologizing when wrong and being willing to forgive each other to move forward. This would help them let go of grudges and build a stronger bond.

Role-Playing Scenarios

Sitting across from each other in their living room, John and Shaveta took turns role-playing different conflict scenarios they had encountered in the past. This exercise would help them apply their newly established ground rules in a safe and controlled environment.

Scenario 1: Project Management Disagreement

John: "Let's say we have a disagreement about the project management approach for a client. How do we handle it without involving a third party?"

Shaveta: "I think it's important to first outline our individual approaches and then discuss the pros and cons of each. We need to listen to each other and find a middle ground."

John: "Agreed. Let's also make sure we focus on the client's needs and the project goals rather than our personal preferences. That should help us stay objective."

Shaveta: "Great point. And if we feel stuck, we could take a break and come back to the discussion with fresh perspectives."

Scenario 2: Workload Imbalance

Shaveta: "Imagine we have a situation where one of us feels overwhelmed with work while the other seems to have a lighter load. How do we handle it?"

John: "We need to openly communicate about our workloads. Maybe we can redistribute tasks or help each other out during particularly busy periods."

Shaveta: "Yes, and we should regularly check in with each other to ensure the workload remains balanced. If one of us feels overwhelmed, we should speak up before it becomes a bigger issue."

John: "Exactly. Regular check-ins will help us stay on top of things and adjust as needed."

Scenario 3: Household Responsibilities During Busy Times

Shaveta: "There was that period when I was swamped with work, and you had to pick up extra household responsibilities. How did you feel about that?"

John: "It was a bit overwhelming, but I knew you were busy. Let's use our strategy to talk about it."

Shaveta: "I feel guilty when you have to do more chores because of my work. How can we balance it better?"

John: "I understand your situation. Maybe we can plan our chores better, or even consider hiring help during particularly busy times."

Shaveta: "That's a good idea. Planning ahead will definitely help us manage better."

Scenario 4: Work-Life Balance During Busy Periods

Shaveta: "Remember when I had that major project deadline, and you felt neglected because I was working late every night?"

John: "Yes, I remember feeling a bit lonely and disconnected. Let's address it."

Shaveta: "I feel pressured to meet my work deadlines, but I also feel guilty for not spending enough time with you. How can we balance this?"

John: "I understand your work pressure. How about we set aside some time each evening, even if it's just 30 minutes, to connect and relax together?"

Shaveta: "I think that's a great idea. It would help me unwind and make sure we stay connected."

Scenario 5: Personal Time vs. Work Commitments

John: "What if we have a conflict about balancing personal time with work commitments? How do we resolve it ourselves?"

Shaveta: "We need to respect each other's need for personal time and ensure we're both making an effort to balance work and life. We could schedule specific times for work and personal activities."

John: "And if a work commitment arises during personal time, we should discuss it and find a way to accommodate both. Flexibility and understanding are key."

Shaveta: "Absolutely. We can also plan ahead to avoid last-minute conflicts and ensure we're both on the same page."

Scenario 6: Differing Opinions on Business Decisions

Shaveta: "Suppose we disagree on a major business decision, like taking on a new client or project. How do we handle that?"

John: "We should lay out all the facts and potential outcomes, then discuss our opinions openly. It's important to listen to each other and consider all angles."

Shaveta: "Maybe we can create a pros and cons list for each decision. That way, we have a clear view of the potential impacts and can make a more informed choice together."

John: "Good idea. And if we still can't agree, we could agree to revisit the decision after some time or set specific criteria to help us decide."

Scenario 7: Personal vs. Professional Boundaries

John: "How about when our personal relationship conflicts with our professional work? How do we handle it without bringing in someone else?"

Shaveta: "We should remind ourselves to keep personal feelings out of professional decisions. Setting clear boundaries will help us manage this."

John: "And if personal feelings do interfere, we should address them outside of work hours to prevent them from affecting our professional roles."

Shaveta: "Exactly. Having a designated time to discuss personal matters will help keep our professional interactions smooth."

By role-playing these scenarios, John and Shaveta reinforced their commitment to resolving conflicts independently. They recognized the importance of communication, empathy, and collaboration in managing disputes. This approach not only strengthened their relationship but also enhanced their problem-solving skills, ensuring they could navigate both personal and professional challenges together without the need for external intervention.

Trust and Dependability

The role-playing scenarios had left John and Shaveta exhausted. They decided to wrap things up and get on with their lives. While they were very happy with their overall dynamics and all the wonderful things they had discovered about each other over the past several weeks, there was one final aspect that needed to be explored to cement their partnership: trust and dependability.

A few days later, after they had both had time to recharge, John and Shaveta sat down to discuss trust and dependability. They knew that these were foundational elements for both their personal and professional relationship.

John: "Trust and dependability are crucial for us to succeed, both as partners and as business collaborators. How do you think we should approach this?"

Shaveta: "I think we need to start by being completely honest with each other about our expectations and any concerns we have. It's important to know that we can rely on each other no matter what."

John: "Agreed. Let's also talk about our past experiences with trust and what has worked or not worked for us."

They began by exploring and discussing the core foundational components of building trust and dependability. This exercise helped them understand each other's expectations and how they approached trust and dependability.

Building Trust

Honesty and Transparency – Open Communication:

They both agreed that honesty and transparency were non-negotiable. They would always tell each other the truth, even if it was difficult.

John: "We need to be open about our thoughts and feelings. If something is bothering us, we should talk about it immediately instead of letting it fester."

Shaveta: "Absolutely. Keeping things inside only leads to misunderstandings and resentment. We should make a pact to always be upfront with each other."

John: "We need to be upfront about everything, even if it's difficult. It's better to address issues head-on than let them fester."

Shaveta: "Agreed. Transparency is the foundation of trust."

Keeping Commitments – Consistency & Reliability:

They recognized that keeping commitments was essential for building trust.

Shaveta: "If we say we're going to do something, we need to follow through. It's important to show that we can depend on each other."

John: "Yes, and if something comes up that prevents us from keeping a commitment, we need to communicate that as soon as possible."

Support and Dependability – Being There for Each Other:

Being supportive and reliable was another key component they identified.

John: "We should always be there for each other, whether it's a work-related issue or a personal matter. Knowing that we have each other's backs is crucial."

Shaveta: "And we need to show appreciation for each other's support. Acknowledging and valuing the other person's efforts strengthens trust."

Shaveta: "Let's have weekly check-ins to make sure we're on track with our commitments."

John: "Good idea. It will help us stay accountable."

Being Vulnerable and Practicing Empathy

They understood that being vulnerable with each other was necessary for building deep trust. This meant sharing fears, insecurities, and mistakes. They also committed to practicing empathy, trying to understand each other's perspectives and feelings.

John: "We should feel safe to be vulnerable with each other. It's important to share our true selves."

Shaveta: "I agree. Vulnerability fosters deeper connection and trust."

Shaveta: "We need to be empathetic and put ourselves in each other's shoes. Understanding each other's emotions is key."

John: "Absolutely! Empathy helps us connect and trust each other more."

When John and Shaveta were finally done with their sessions, they felt a renewed sense of closeness and understanding. They appreciated each other more and had built a strong relationship that could be simply described as the dynamics of two best friends who worked together. Their bond had grown stronger, and their mutual respect and trust laid the foundation for a successful partnership.

With newfound confidence and clarity, they decided to take a bold step forward. They formed a partnership company and began their entrepreneurial journey as a team. By honing into each other's strengths, they became a force to be reckoned with in their field. John's analytical prowess and problem-solving skills complemented Shaveta's strategic vision and technical expertise. Together, they tackled projects with precision and creativity, offering clients innovative solutions that exceeded expectations.

The days passed quickly as they delivered one project after another. Each success fueled their ambition, and they found joy in celebrating their milestones together. Their professional synergy translated into efficient workflows and outstanding results, earning them a reputation for excellence.

Clients appreciated their collaborative approach and the seamless way they integrated their skills to provide comprehensive solutions. They navigated challenges with ease, drawing on their shared experiences and the trust they had built during their initial sessions.

Their partnership wasn't just about business; it was about a shared dream and the excitement of building something meaningful together. The respect they had for each other's abilities and the support they provided during tough times solidified their partnership.

As they continued to grow their business, John and Shaveta knew that their journey was just beginning.

They had created a powerful dynamic that would sustain them through any challenges ahead. Together, they looked forward to a future filled with opportunities, confident in their ability to achieve great things as a team.

Their partnership flourished as they took on more complex and rewarding projects. With each new challenge, John and Shaveta found ways to innovate and push the boundaries of their expertise. Their company began to attract attention from larger clients, and soon, they were handling high-profile projects that demanded their combined skills and creativity.

John's analytical mind continued to dissect problems with precision, while Shaveta's strategic thinking helped them navigate through intricate project requirements. Their complementary skills made them a formidable team, and their clients soon recognized the value they brought to the table.

One of their most significant projects involved revamping the IT infrastructure for a well-known corporation. The project was massive in scope and complexity, but John and Shaveta approached it with their usual meticulous planning and teamwork. They held brainstorming sessions to map out the project's phases, ensuring that every detail was accounted for.

During the project, their ability to communicate openly and trust each other's judgment proved invaluable. When unexpected challenges arose, they tackled them head-on, using the conflict resolution techniques they had practiced. Their resilience and ability to adapt quickly impressed their clients and further solidified their reputation in the industry.

As the months went by, their business continued to grow. They began to hire a team of talented individuals who shared their vision and work ethic. John and Shaveta took on leadership roles, mentoring their employees and fostering a collaborative and innovative work environment. They encouraged their team to take initiative, share ideas, and approach problems creatively.

Despite the increasing demands of their business, John and Shaveta never lost sight of their personal relationship. They made time for each other, ensuring that their bond remained strong. They enjoyed simple pleasures like cooking dinner together, going for long walks, and sharing their dreams for the future.

One evening, after a particularly successful project completion, they sat together on their balcony, looking out at the city lights.

John: "We've come a long way, haven't we?"

Shaveta: "We really have. I'm so proud of what we've achieved together."

John: "And it's only the beginning. There's so much more we can do."

Shaveta: "Absolutely. I can't wait to see where our journey takes us next."

Their entrepreneurial journey was a testament to their hard work, dedication, and the strength of their partnership. They had proven that with mutual respect, trust, and a shared vision, they could overcome any challenge and achieve great success.

As they continued to build their business, they remained committed to their core values of integrity, innovation, and collaboration. They knew that their success was not just measured by the projects they completed but by the relationships they built and the positive impact they made on their clients and their team.

John and Shaveta's story was one of love, partnership, and the relentless pursuit of excellence. They had found not only professional success but also personal fulfillment in each other. Together, they looked forward to a future filled with endless possibilities, ready to tackle whatever came their way, hand in hand.

Author's Note

The points and scenarios articulated in this chapter are used as examples only. It is nearly impossible to identify all potential scenarios that you may encounter in your personal and professional relationships. It is important to understand that this is not a psychology book. Every human being is unique, and their ability to react and deal with certain scenarios varies significantly.

While I have used some examples and techniques in a unique format involving a couple who are also in a professional relationship, it is crucial to appreciate that these dynamics can be replicated in several other relationship types. The interactions and conflicts between John and Shaveta serve as illustrative examples rather than prescriptive solutions.

The techniques and strategies discussed in this book are intended to provide basic guidelines. They are not exhaustive and should not be taken as one-size-fits-all solutions. Instead, I encourage you to use these scenarios as a starting point and adapt them to your own unique circumstances.

Remember, you can always come up with your own tricks and techniques when navigating various aspects of your personal and professional dynamics with someone. The key is to maintain open communication, empathy, and a willingness to work through challenges together.

I hope that the insights shared in this book inspire you to reflect on your own relationships and develop personalized strategies that work best for you. Thank you for joining me on this journey through the intricate world of personal and professional relationships. Your ability to adapt and grow in these areas is a testament to your commitment to building meaningful and lasting connections.

Warm regards,

Anupamm Singh

Chapter 11

Hindsight is Never 20/20

Five years had passed since John and Shaveta embarked on their entrepreneurial journey. Their company had grown significantly, and they were now well-known figures within the industry. Their expertise and innovative solutions had earned them numerous accolades and a loyal client base. However, their most cherished accomplishments were not just professional but deeply personal. John and Shaveta were now the proud parents of two beautiful girls, Prisha and Riya.

The arrival of their daughters brought immense joy and a new set of challenges. Balancing the demands of a thriving business with the responsibilities of parenthood required careful planning and adjustments. They were determined to restructure their personal and professional lives to suit their current situation and ensure they provided the best for their family.

Restructuring Their Professional Lives

To accommodate their new roles as parents, John and Shaveta decided to delegate more responsibilities within their company. They promoted key team members to leadership positions, entrusting them with greater autonomy in managing projects and clients. This not only allowed John and Shaveta to focus on strategic decisions but also empowered their team, fostering a culture of trust and collaboration.

John: "We've built an incredible team. It's time we let them take on more responsibility. We can focus on guiding them and making sure the company continues to grow."

Shaveta: "Absolutely. Delegating will give us the time we need to be present for Prisha and Riya. We can still oversee everything without being involved in the day-to-day operations."

Creating a Family-Friendly Work Environment

Recognizing the importance of work-life balance, they implemented family-friendly policies within their company. Flexible working hours, remote work options, and a dedicated family room in the office allowed employees, including themselves, to balance their professional and personal commitments more effectively.

Shaveta: "We should create an environment where parents feel supported. If we make these changes, it will benefit not just us but everyone in the company."

John: "Agreed. A happy and balanced team will be more productive and committed. It's a win-win for everyone."

Prioritizing Personal Time

Despite their busy schedules, John and Shaveta made a conscious effort to prioritize personal time. They established a routine that allowed them to spend quality time with their daughters, ensuring they were present for important milestones and everyday moments alike.

John: "Let's make sure we have family dinners every night. No work distractions, just us and the girls."

Shaveta: "And weekends should be family time. We can take the girls to the park, go on trips, or just spend time at home together."

John often found himself reflecting on the twists and turns of his life, marvelling at the journey that had brought him to where he was. Sitting in his cozy study, surrounded by the warmth of his family and the success of his professional endeavours, he couldn't help but feel a deep sense of gratitude. Shaveta, his partner in life and business, had been a cornerstone of his journey, and their daughters, Prisha and Riya, filled their lives with joy and purpose. He often thanked God for the blessings he had received, acknowledging the divine hand that seemed to guide him through life's challenges.

Reflecting on Alternate Career Paths

Despite his contentment, John was an introspective thinker who often pondered the "what ifs" of life. He imagined different scenarios, wondering how his life might have unfolded under various circumstances. Each hypothetical path offered a unique set of experiences and lessons, and John found himself daydreaming about these alternate realities during quiet moments.

One afternoon, as he sat by the window of his apartment, watching the city bustle below, John let his mind wander. What if he had pursued his childhood dream of becoming an architect? He envisioned himself sketching blueprints and overseeing the construction of towering skyscrapers. He imagined the satisfaction of seeing his designs come to life, each building a testament to his creativity and precision. He saw himself working late nights in a sleek office, surrounded by models and drawings, driven by the passion to create structures that would define city skylines.

In another scenario, John pictured himself as a writer. What if he had followed his love for storytelling and written novels? He imagined days spent in cozy cafes, tapping away at his laptop, lost in the worlds he created. His mind filled with characters and plots, each story an exploration of the human experience. He saw himself attending book signings and literary festivals, engaging with readers who found solace and inspiration in his words. The idea of touching people's lives through stories gave him a sense of profound fulfillment.

John also wondered about the road not taken in academia. What if he had become a professor? He envisioned himself lecturing in grand halls filled with eager students, sharing his knowledge and sparking intellectual curiosity. He imagined mentoring young minds, guiding them through their academic journeys, and conducting research that could contribute to his field of study. The thought of shaping the next generation of thinkers and innovators brought a smile to his face.

These daydreams extended to personal decisions as well. What if he had moved to a different city or even a different country? He pictured himself living in a bustling metropolis like New York or a serene coastal town in Europe. Each location offered a different lifestyle and set of adventures. He imagined making new friends, exploring unfamiliar places, and immersing himself in different cultures. The excitement of starting anew and the thrill of discovery filled him with a sense of wonder.

John's introspective nature also led him to consider the relationships he had formed. What if he had maintained closer ties with certain friends or pursued a different romantic relationship? He thought about the people who had come into his life and the impact they had on him. Each relationship, whether it lasted or faded, taught him valuable lessons about love, trust, and connection. He pondered how different choices might have led to different outcomes, shaping his personal growth in unique ways.

These reflections were not about regret or dissatisfaction but rather a deep curiosity about the myriad possibilities that life offered. John understood that every decision he made set him on a path that was uniquely his own. He appreciated the experiences and lessons his current journey provided, but he also found joy in imagining the roads less travelled.

As an introspective thinker, John knew that these "what if" scenarios were part of his nature. They allowed him to explore the depths of his desires and aspirations, even those that remained unfulfilled. They also served as a reminder of the infinite possibilities that life held, each with its own set of challenges and rewards.

Despite his contentment, these musings kept him grounded and open to new opportunities. They encouraged him to embrace change and take risks, knowing that each decision could lead to unexpected and enriching experiences. John cherished the life he had built but remained excited about the unknown future, filled with potential and the promise of continued growth.

In moments of quiet reflection, John found a delicate balance between appreciating his present and dreaming about his future. This introspection fuelled his motivation to make the most of every opportunity and to continuously seek fulfillment in all aspects of his life. With a heart full of gratitude and a mind open to endless possibilities, John navigated his journey with a sense of purpose and wonder, ready to embrace whatever paths lay ahead.

The What-If Conundrum

As John sat in his study, the quiet hum of the evening offering a perfect backdrop for contemplation. The flicker of his desk lamp cast a soft glow on his face as he pondered, "What if I had continued working for my old company instead of pursuing my dreams?" At the time he left, he was already a Senior Systems Analyst, and the decision to leave was daunting yet exhilarating. But what if he had stayed? He imagined himself exploring various divisions and roles within the familiar environment. Two natural career paths stood out: Project Manager and Solutions Architect.

John as a Project Manager

In his mind's eye, John visualised himself stepping into the role of a Project Manager. He would have managed a diverse array of responsibilities, including people, finances, risks, issues, and stakeholders. The role demanded a high level of coordination and oversight, ensuring that projects were delivered on time and within budget. John imagined leading a team of analysts, developers, and testers, orchestrating their efforts to achieve common goals. He would have been responsible for creating detailed project plans, defining scopes, and setting realistic timelines. His days would be filled with meetings, from kick-off sessions to progress reviews, and he would need to keep a constant pulse on the project's health.

John knew his strong leadership and organizational skills would serve him well in this role. He envisioned himself mitigating risks, resolving issues, and managing stakeholders' expectations. His ability to communicate effectively with different departments and his knack for problem-solving would be crucial in navigating the complexities of project management. However, John also realized the potential challenges. The less hands-on nature of the role concerned him. He enjoyed diving into the technical details, understanding the intricacies of systems and data. As a Project Manager, his focus would shift more towards administrative and managerial tasks. The day-to-day responsibilities would involve more planning and oversight rather than direct involvement in problem-solving.

Over time, John feared he might feel disconnected from the technical aspects that he loved. The focus on budgets, schedules, and resource allocation could overshadow his passion for technology and innovation. He worried that the administrative burdens might lead to a gradual loss of interest in his work. John also pondered the impact on his creativity. As a hands-on analyst and consultant, he thrived on finding innovative solutions to complex problems. The structured and process-oriented nature of project management might stifle this creativity. He imagined himself longing for the days when he could immerse himself in the technical challenges that fuelled his passion.

As John contemplated this path, he realized that while he had the skills to excel as a Project Manager, the role might not bring him the same level of satisfaction. The distance from hands-on work and the shift towards managerial responsibilities could diminish his enthusiasm over time. John also thought about the personal impact of this career choice. The demanding nature of project management could affect his work-life balance. The constant pressure to deliver projects on time and manage stakeholder expectations might lead to long hours and increased stress. He wondered how this would affect his personal life and relationships.

In his introspection, John found a renewed appreciation for the path he had chosen. His freelance journey allowed him to stay true to his passion for problem-solving and maintain a balance between technical work and project management. He enjoyed the freedom to choose projects that aligned with his interests and the opportunity to work closely with clients and teams. John's reflections reaffirmed his belief that every career path has its own set of challenges and rewards. While the role of a Project Manager offered stability and growth, it might not have fulfilled his desire for hands-on technical work and creativity. His decision to pursue freelancing allowed him to create a fulfilling career that resonated with his passion and strengths.

John as a Solution Architect

As John continued his introspection and exploring other What-If scenarios, the thought of becoming a Solutions Architect intrigued him deeply.

He envisaged himself stepping into the role of a Solution Architect. The position was heavily focused on technology, which was a domain he had always been passionate about. He would have been responsible for designing and implementing complex IT solutions, ensuring they met the business requirements and integrated seamlessly with existing systems. He imagined himself working closely with internal clients to understand their needs, then translating those needs into technical specifications and architectural designs.

John envisioned his days filled with high-level discussions about technology stacks, software architecture, and system integrations. He would collaborate with development teams, guiding them through the implementation process and ensuring that the solutions aligned with the architectural vision. His expertise in various technologies would be the cornerstone of his role, allowing him to craft innovative solutions to meet complex business challenges.

However, as he delved deeper into this imagined scenario, John realized the potential drawbacks. The role of a Solution Architect was intensely focused on technology. While this was exciting, it also meant he might lose touch with the process and people aspects of projects that he enjoyed. The hands-on problem-solving and direct interactions with diverse teams, which had always been a source of satisfaction for him, would be replaced by a more strategic and high-level approach.

John also contemplated the impact on his creativity. As a hands-on analyst and consultant, he thrived on finding innovative solutions to complex problems by understanding the nuances of both technology and business processes. The structured nature of the Solution Architect role might limit his ability to engage in the holistic problem-solving approach he loved. He worried that focusing solely on the technical side could make his work feel one-dimensional.

The more John thought about this path, the more he realized that while he had the technical skills to excel as a Solution Architect, the role might not provide the same level of personal fulfillment. The distance from the process and people aspects could diminish his enthusiasm over time. He valued the balance of technology, process, and interpersonal interactions in his work, which a Solution Architect role might not fully offer.

John's introspection also led him to consider the personal impact of this career choice. The demanding nature of high-level technical roles could affect his work-life balance. The constant pressure to stay updated with the latest technological advancements and ensure flawless system integrations might lead to long hours and increased stress. He wondered how this would affect his personal life and relationships.

As he pondered these alternative scenarios, John found a renewed appreciation for the path he had chosen. His freelance journey allowed him to stay true to his passion for problem-solving, blending technical work with process improvements and client interactions. He enjoyed the freedom to choose projects that aligned with his interests and the opportunity to work closely with clients and teams.

John's reflections reaffirmed his belief that every career path has its own set of challenges and rewards. While the role of a Solution Architect offered stability and growth in the technology domain, it might not have fulfilled his desire for a balanced approach to problem-solving. His decision to pursue freelancing allowed him to create a fulfilling career that resonated with his passion and strengths.

Would John have Met Shaveta?

As John sat in his cozy study, and continued reflecting on the twists and turns of his life, he wondered about the possibility of meeting Shaveta if he had stayed at his old company. The circumstances that led to their first encounter were so unique and fortuitous that it seemed almost impossible to replicate in another setting. Shaveta's path had crossed his at a critical juncture in his life, leading to both personal and professional fulfillment. John vividly recalled the moment they met near the reception of a large corporate client's office building, how their collaboration blossomed into a partnership, and eventually into a deep, loving relationship.

John imagined what his life might have been like if he had remained in his old company. Would he and Shaveta have ever met? Perhaps their paths could have crossed at a conference or industry event, but John questioned whether they would have ended up together. The dynamics of their meeting, collaboration, and eventual partnership were deeply influenced by the circumstances of his freelance journey. It was during his freelancing days that he had the freedom and flexibility to explore new opportunities, which led him to the client office where they met.

Even if their paths had crossed in a different setting, John pondered whether the same bond would have formed between them. The shared experience of building a business together, overcoming challenges, and celebrating successes had strengthened their relationship. Their connection grew out of late-night brainstorming sessions, joint client meetings, and the shared goal of creating something meaningful together. Would those same dynamics have been present if he had stayed in a more traditional career path, tied to the routines and structures of his old company?

John's mind drifted to a conversation he had with Shaveta recently. They were sitting on their balcony, watching their daughters play in the park below. Shaveta asked him, "Do you ever wonder what our lives would be like if you hadn't left your old job?" John smiled, looking at her. "I do," he admitted. "But every time I think about it, I realize how lucky I am to have taken the leap. Meeting you, starting our business, it all feels like it was meant to be."

In that moment, John felt a profound sense of gratitude for the path he had chosen. The decision to leave his old company had led him to Shaveta, and together they had built a life that was rich with love, purpose, and shared dreams. He couldn't imagine his life without her, and he knew that their journey together was the result of a series of deliberate choices and fortunate events.

Reflecting on the possibility of not meeting Shaveta made John appreciate their bond even more. Their relationship had been forged through mutual respect, shared aspirations, and the challenges they faced together. The thought of a life without her made him realize how integral she was to his happiness and success.

John's introspection reaffirmed his belief that some things in life are meant to be. While the path not taken might have offered different opportunities, it was the path he chose that led him to Shaveta. Their partnership, both personal and professional, was a testament to the power of taking risks and following one's heart. John understood that while life is filled with uncertainties, the choices he made had brought him to a place of contentment and fulfillment that he wouldn't trade for anything.

Reflecting on these alternative scenarios, John's introspection brought him a sense of peace. The more he tried to visualize these other possibilities and paths, the more confident he became that the path he had chosen was the one meant for him. Every scenario he imagined had its own set of challenges and rewards, but there was no way of knowing with certainty that any other path would have led to a more content and happier destination. He understood that life is filled with uncertainties, and every decision shapes our journey in unique ways.

Conclusion

John's introspections reaffirmed his gratitude for the present. The what-ifs and alternate paths highlighted the significance of his choices and the blessings he had received. As he pondered these alternate realities, he came to understand that each potential path had its own set of challenges and rewards. However, the path he had chosen, guided by love and partnership with Shaveta, brought him a unique and irreplaceable fulfillment.

Reflecting on his journey from a Graduate Business Analyst to a seasoned professional and entrepreneur, John recognized several points of enlightenment that had shaped his life. These moments of clarity and understanding had been pivotal in his personal and professional development, guiding him through challenges and helping him appreciate the blessings in his life.

One of the earliest moments of enlightenment came during his first project as a Graduate Business Analyst. John had been overwhelmed by the complexity of the tasks and the high expectations placed on him. It was when he received his first meeting invitation from Process Peters, that he realized the importance of asking the right questions. This insight transformed his approach to problem-solving and became a foundational skill throughout his career.

Meeting Shaveta was another profound turning point. Her presence in his life brought not only love and companionship but also a partnership that enriched his professional journey. Together, they navigated the challenges of entrepreneurship, each bringing unique strengths to the table. John's enlightenment here was understanding the power of collaboration and the incredible impact of a supportive partner.

John's decision to leave his corporate job and start his own business was driven by another moment of clarity. He realized that true fulfillment came from pursuing his passion and creating something meaningful. The initial struggles of entrepreneurship taught him resilience and adaptability. He learned that failure was not the end but a stepping stone to success. This understanding allowed him to embrace risks and view setbacks as opportunities for growth.

The experience of building a team from the ground up provided John with another significant insight. He discovered the joy of nurturing talent and seeing his team members thrive. This realization deepened his appreciation for leadership and the responsibility it carried. He learned that a great leader inspires and empowers others, fostering an environment where everyone can contribute their best.

John's interactions with clients and customers brought yet another layer of enlightenment. He found immense satisfaction in knowing that his work made a real difference in their lives. Listening to their feedback and continuously improving his products reinforced the importance of customer-centric innovation. This perspective kept him grounded and motivated, ensuring that his business always aligned with the needs of those it served.

Through all these experiences, John also learned the importance of balance. There were times when he was so consumed by his work that he neglected his health and personal relationships. Shaveta's gentle reminders and their shared moments of reflection helped him understand that true success included personal well-being and happiness. This balance became a guiding principle in both his life and his business practices.

Reflecting on the alternate path of being a solo entrepreneur, John realized the immense difference Shaveta had made. Without her, he might have succeeded eventually, but the journey would have been lonelier and more arduous. The joy of shared success, the comfort of mutual support during tough times, and the profound sense of partnership were irreplaceable aspects of his life with Shaveta.

The "what ifs" served as a powerful reminder of the significance of his choices and the blessings he had received. They highlighted how different his life could have been, emphasizing the importance of the love and support he had found with Shaveta and their family. Every hypothetical scenario underscored the fact that his current path, with its unique blend of personal and professional fulfillment, was exactly where he wanted to be.

John's gratitude extended beyond his partnership with Shaveta. He was thankful for the life they had built together, including their children, their home, and the countless memories they had created. Family dinners filled with laughter, vacations that brought them closer, and the simple, everyday moments of joy and connection all contributed to his deep sense of contentment.

He also appreciated the professional successes they had achieved together. Their startup had grown from a small venture into a thriving business, making a tangible difference in the lives of their clients. The team they had built felt more like a family, united by a shared vision and values. Every milestone reached was a testament to their hard work, dedication, and the synergy of their partnership.

With a heart full of gratitude and a mind at peace, John looked forward to the future. He was ready to embrace whatever came next, confident that with Shaveta by his side, they could face any challenge and cherish every moment. He knew that life's journey could take many forms, and while the paths might be different, the constants of love, support, and shared dreams made his life truly fulfilling.

As he gazed out the window at the bustling city below, John felt a profound sense of serenity. The future was uncertain, but that uncertainty no longer filled him with apprehension. Instead, it was a source of excitement and possibility. He was eager to continue growing, learning, and experiencing life's wonders, knowing that every step of the way, Shaveta would be there with him.

Together, they had built a life rich in love and purpose. John's introspections had reaffirmed what he already knew deep down: that the journey he was on, with all its ups and downs, was the right one for him. He felt blessed to have Shaveta as his partner, and he was ready to embrace the future, hand in hand with the person who had made his life so incredibly fulfilling.

With renewed determination and a heart brimming with gratitude, John embraced the challenges and opportunities that lay ahead. He was ready to face whatever the future held, knowing that with Shaveta by his side, they could overcome any obstacle and savour every moment of their shared journey.

As John reflected on his journey, from a Graduate Business Analyst to a successful entrepreneur, he realized that each step had been a lesson in resilience, love, and self-discovery. These moments of enlightenment had shaped him into the person he was today, and he looked forward to the future with hope and excitement, ready to embrace the unknown with the love of his life by his side.

THE END

www.ingramcontent.com/pod-product-compliance
Lightning Source LLC
Chambersburg PA
CBHW031524150726
47990CB00001B/49